A Festive Christmas

Wonderful Ideas for Decorating, Cooking & Gift Giving

CREATIVE
PUBLISHING
international

MINNETONKA, MINNESOTA

CONTENTS

Copyright © 1997
Creative Publishing international, Inc.
5900 Green Oak Drive
Minnetonka, Minnesota 55343
1-800-328-3895
All rights reserved
Printed in U.S.A.

Library of Congress
Cataloging-in-Publication Data

A festive Christmas : wonderful ideas for
decorating, cooking & gift giving.
    p.   cm.
  ISBN 0-86573-192-6 (softcover)
  1. Christmas decorations. 2. Christmas
  cookery. I. Creative Publishing international, Inc.
TT900.C4F47 1997
745.594'12--dc21   97-13374

CREATIVE
PUBLISHING
international

President: Iain Macfarlane
Group Director, Book Development:
Zoe Graul

Created by: The Editors of
Creative Publishing international, Inc.
Printed on American paper by:
R. R. Donnelley & Sons Co.
02 01 00 99 98 / 6 5 4 3 2

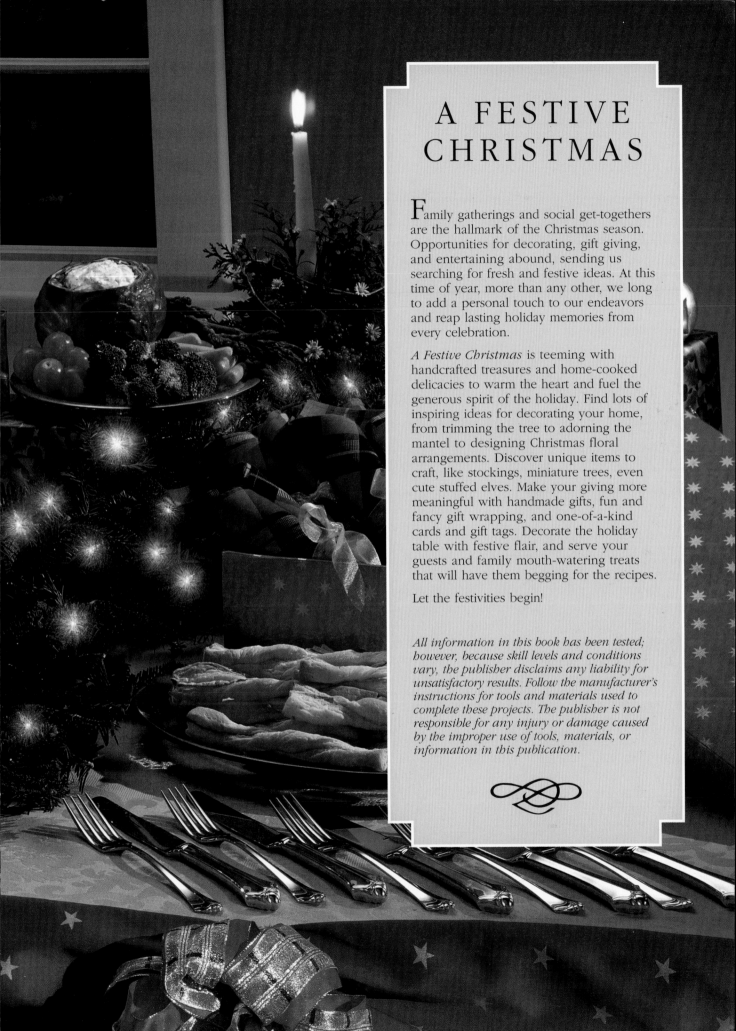

A FESTIVE CHRISTMAS

Family gatherings and social get-togethers are the hallmark of the Christmas season. Opportunities for decorating, gift giving, and entertaining abound, sending us searching for fresh and festive ideas. At this time of year, more than any other, we long to add a personal touch to our endeavors and reap lasting holiday memories from every celebration.

A Festive Christmas is teeming with handcrafted treasures and home-cooked delicacies to warm the heart and fuel the generous spirit of the holiday. Find lots of inspiring ideas for decorating your home, from trimming the tree to adorning the mantel to designing Christmas floral arrangements. Discover unique items to craft, like stockings, miniature trees, even cute stuffed elves. Make your giving more meaningful with handmade gifts, fun and fancy gift wrapping, and one-of-a-kind cards and gift tags. Decorate the holiday table with festive flair, and serve your guests and family mouth-watering treats that will have them begging for the recipes.

Let the festivities begin!

Decorating
The Tree

TREE TRIMMING

Collectible metal toys and cookie cutters *are used as ornaments to create a country-style tree. Popcorn garland and fabric bows are used for contrast, and raffia streamers add to the country look.*

A variety of ornaments can be mixed successfully on a tree. Create a unified look by emphasizing a particular color or style, repeating it in several areas of the tree. For interest, add a few elements of surprise, such as an artificial bird's nest, oversize decorations, dried or silk flowers, or raffia streamers.

Wired-ribbon bow *is used as a tree topper. Streamers of ribbon cascade down the tree and are tucked into the branches. Gold and bronze foliage and berry picks are tucked into the branches to complete the elegant look.*

Dried floral materials, *such as baby's breath, German statice, roses, and pepper berries, are tucked into the tree, creating a garland effect. Several craft bird's nests and birds add to the natural look. Dried flowers, tied with a bow, are used as a tree topper.*

Artificial fruit garland *gives a natural look to this tree. Aromatic dried-fruit-slice ornaments (pages 44 and 45) and honeysuckle vine are used to decorate the tree.*

Oversize decorations, *such as snowmen, can be used for impact on a tree. Place the oversize decorations on the tree first, securing them with floral wire, if necessary. Candy canes and frosted twigs are used to fill in bare areas.*

TREE TOPPERS

A tree topper adds the finishing touch to a Christmas tree. Select one that coordinates with the style or theme of the ornaments, such as a paper-twist angel to complement a tree with a homespun look. Make a wire-mesh bow to top a tree that is decorated with glittery or metallic objects, or make a cinnamon-stick star for a tree decorated with natural ornaments.

The angel shown opposite is crafted from paper twist, a tightly wrapped paper cording that, when untwisted, produces a crinkled paper strip. The angel is given dimension with the help of wire. The outline of the wings is shaped from paper twist with a wire inner core, and the garment and shawl have craft wire encased in the fold of the hems, allowing them to be shaped into drapes and folds. Embellish the angel as desired with a miniature artificial garland or tiny musical instrument.

For an elegant-looking tree topper, create a large wire-mesh bow from aluminum window screening. The window screening, available in shiny silver and dull charcoal gray, may be left unfinished or painted gold, brass, or copper. The bow may also be sprayed with aerosol glitter for added sparkle.

For a natural look, make a star from cinnamon sticks held together with hot glue and raffia. The star can be embellished with a raffia bow, miniature cones, and a few sprigs of greenery.

Angel (opposite) is created from paper twist, sinamay ribbon, jute, and raffia, for a country look.

Wire-mesh bow, *created from window screening, is sprayed with gold metallic paint for an elegant look.*

Cinnamon-stick star *is embellished with sprigs of greenery, red raffia, and miniature cones.*

11

HOW TO MAKE A PAPER-TWIST ANGEL TREE TOPPER

MATERIALS

- Poster board.
- Packing tape.
- Three 1½" (3.8 cm) Styrofoam® balls.
- ½ yd. (0.5 m) paper twist, 4" to 4½" (10 to 11.5 cm) wide, in skintone or natural color, for head, neck, and hands.
- 1 yd. (0.95 m) paper twist, 4" to 4½" (10 to 11.5 cm) wide, for shawl.
- 2 yd. (1.85 m) paper twist, 7" to 7½" (18 to 19.3 cm) wide, for dress.

- 1 yd. (0.95 m) paper twist with wire inner core, for wings.
- Sinamay ribbon, at least 2" (5 cm) wide, for wings.
- Raffia.
- 3-ply jute.
- Dowel, ⅛" (3 mm) in diameter.
- 24-gauge craft wire.
- Thick craft glue.
- Hot glue gun and glue sticks.
- Wire cutter or utility scissors.
- Miniature garland or other desired embellishments.

CUTTING DIRECTIONS

From skintone or natural paper twist, cut one 4" (10 cm) piece for the head, one 10" (25 cm) piece for the underbodice, and three ¾" (2 cm) pieces for the neck and hands.

From the paper twist for the dress, cut two 4½" (11.5 cm) pieces for the sleeves, six 8½" (21.8 cm) pieces for the skirt, and one 7" (18 cm) piece for the dress bodice.

From the paper twist with a wire inner core, cut one 12" (30.5 cm) length for the arms and one 24" (61 cm) length for the wings.

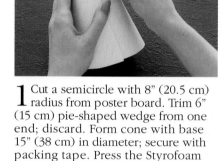

1 Cut a semicircle with 8" (20.5 cm) radius from poster board. Trim 6" (15 cm) pie-shaped wedge from one end; discard. Form cone with base 15" (38 cm) in diameter; secure with packing tape. Press the Styrofoam balls between fingers to compress to 1¼" (3.2 cm) in diameter.

2 Untwist paper twist for head; glue width of paper around Styrofoam ball, using craft glue. Apply craft glue to ball at top and bottom, and tightly retwist paper; apply additional glue as necessary so paper stays twisted. Allow glue to dry.

3 Trim one end of the twisted paper close to foam ball; this will be top of head. Poke remaining twisted end into top of cone; trim top of cone, if necessary. Remove head, and set aside.

4 Poke a hole through each side of the cone, 1" (2.5 cm) from top; for the arms, insert the paper twist with the wire inner core through the holes. Push each wire arm through the center of Styrofoam ball; for shoulders, slide balls up to the cone. Shape balls to fit snugly against cone by pressing with fingers; secure to cone with hot glue, applying the glue to the cone.

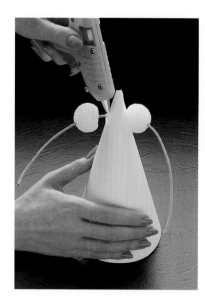

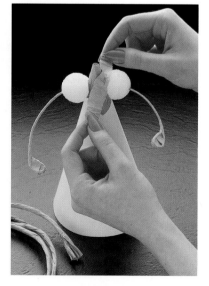

5 Bend each wire arm 1" (2.5 cm) from end; bend to form triangle shape for hands. Untwist a paper strip for hand; mist it with water. Wrap paper around the hand; secure with craft glue. Repeat for the other hand. Untwist and mist the paper strip for neck. Wrap paper around top of cone; secure with craft glue.

6 Untwist underbodice piece; cut a small slit in center. Position slit in paper over top of cone; smooth paper around shoulders and cone. Secure with craft glue. Glue head in place.

7 Untwist skirt pieces. Join the skirt pieces together by overlapping long edges ¼" (6 mm); secure with glue to form tube. Fold ½" (1.3 cm) hem on one edge; insert wire into fold, overlapping ends of wire about 1" (2.5 cm). Secure hem with craft glue, encasing wire.

8 Place cone on a soup or vegetable can. Slide skirt over cone, with the hem about 2" (5 cm) below the lower edge of the cone. Hand-gather upper edge to fit smoothly around the waist; secure with wire. Shape wired hem into graceful folds.

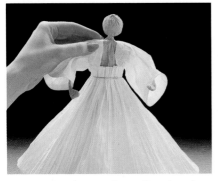

9 Untwist sleeve piece. Overlap the edges ¼" (6 mm) to form a tube; secure with craft glue. Fold the hem, encasing the wire as in step 7. Slide sleeve over arm, placing hem at wrist. Glue sleeve at shoulder, sides, and underarm, concealing underbodice at underarm. Shape wired hem. Repeat for other sleeve.

10 Untwist dress bodice piece; cut in half lengthwise. Fold strips in half lengthwise. Drape one strip over each shoulder, placing folded edges at neck; cross the ends at front and back; glue in place. Wrap wire around waist; trim excess.

11 Cut several lengths of raffia, about 25" (63.5 cm) long; mist with water. Tie raffia around waist, concealing the wire; trim ends. Cut thicker raffia lengths, and separate into two or three strands.

12 Bend the paper twist with wire inner core for wings as shown; allow the ends to extend 1" (2.5 cm) beyond center. Wrap ends around center; secure with glue.

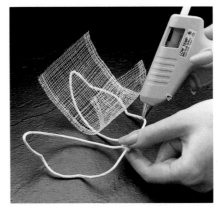

13 Bend edges and curve of wings as shown. Glue sinamay ribbon to back of wings, using hot glue. Allow glue to dry; trim away excess ribbon.

14 Position wings on back of angel at center, so wings curve away from back; secure, using hot glue.

(Continued)

15 Cut jute, and separate to make three single-ply 30" (76 cm) lengths. Wrap each ply tightly and evenly around dowel, securing the ends. Saturate jute with water. Place the dowel in 200°F (95°C) oven for 2 hours or until dry.

16 Remove jute from the dowel. Cut and glue individual lengths of coiled jute to head for hair, working in sections; for the bangs, glue short pieces across the front of the head.

17 Untwist the shawl piece. Fold ½" (1.3 cm) hem on one long edge. Insert wire into fold; glue hem in place, encasing wire. Repeat on opposite side.

18 Drape shawl around the shoulders. Shape the wired hems to make a graceful drape; adjust the shawl in back to conceal the lower portion of the wings. Fold ends of shawl to underside of the skirt. Glue shawl in place in several areas, using hot glue.

19 Shape the wire arms to hold desired accessories. Secure any other embellishments to angel as desired, using hot glue.

HOW TO MAKE A WIRE-MESH BOW TREE TOPPER

MATERIALS

- Aluminum window screening.
- 24-gauge or 26-gauge craft wire.
- Utility scissors.
- Aerosol acrylic paint in metallic finish, optional.
- Aerosol glitter, optional.

CUTTING DIRECTIONS

Cut the following rectangles from window screening, cutting along the mesh weave: one 8" × 38" (20.5 × 96.5 cm) piece for the loops, one 8" × 28" (20.5 × 71 cm) piece for the streamers, and one 2½" × 7" (6.5 × 18 cm) rectangle for the center strip.

1 Paint both sides of each rectangle, if desired; allow to dry. Fold up ½" (1.3 cm) on long edges, using a straightedge as a guide. Fold up ½" (1.3 cm) along short edges of streamers and one short edge of center strip.

2 Cut 16" (40.5 cm) length of wire. Form a loop from rectangle for loops, overlapping the short ends about ¾" (2 cm) at center. Insert wire at one overlapped edge; twist wire to secure, leaving 2" (5 cm) tail.

3 Stitch through the center of overlapped mesh with long end of wire, taking 1" to 1½" (2.5 to 3.8 cm) stitches. Pull up wire firmly to gather mesh; wrap wire around center, and twist the ends together; trim the excess.

4 Hand-pleat width of streamer at the center; place below the gathered loop. Wrap length of wire around the center of loop and streamers; twist ends together. Paint wire to match bow, if necessary.

5 Wrap center strip around the bow, concealing the wire. Stitch ends together with length of wire. Apply aerosol glitter, if desired. Secure a length of wire to the back of center strip for securing bow to tree.

HOW TO MAKE A CINNAMON-STICK STAR TREE TOPPER

MATERIALS

- Five 12" (30.5 cm) cinnamon sticks.
- Hot glue gun and glue sticks.
- Raffia.
- Embellishments, such as cones and sprigs of greenery.

1 Arrange two cinnamon sticks in an "X"; position a third stick across the top, placing one end below upper stick of "X" as shown.

2 Place remaining two sticks on top in an inverted "V." Adjust spacing of cinnamon sticks as necessary, to form star. Secure sticks at ends, using hot glue.

3 Tie raffia securely around ends at intersection of cinnamon sticks. Tie several lengths of raffia into bow; glue to top of star. Secure embellishments with glue.

GARLANDS

Tree garlands can be made in a variety of styles. Shown top to bottom, choose from a rope garland, wrapped ball-and-spool garland, a dried-fruit-slice garland, or a wired-ribbon garland.

For ease in assembling, make the garlands in lengths of about 72" (183 cm). The wired-ribbon garland can be made any length. Most garlands are constructed with loops at the ends for securing the garlands to the branches.

Decorate a tree with a country or natural look, using a rope garland embellished with berry or floral clusters. The clusters may be purchased ready-made, or you can make your own.

To make a wrapped ball-and-spool garland with a country look, wrap torn fabric strips around Styrofoam® balls and wooden spools, then string them together with a piece of jute or twine. Buttons can be added to the garland for more color. Adding buttons decreases the number of wrapped balls and spools needed.

For a dried-fruit-slice garland, combine dried apple and orange slices with cinnamon sticks and fresh cranberries. String the items together with a piece of raffia for a natural look. You can dry your own fruit slices by placing them in a low-temperature oven for several hours. The drying time will vary, depending on the moisture content of the fruit. Remove the fruit slices from the oven when they feel like leather. If the slices are dried too long, they will be brittle and break; if the drying time is too short, they will be soft and spoil. The fresh cranberries will dry naturally on the garland after it is made.

A wired-ribbon garland can be made inexpensively from fabric strips, beading wire, and paper-backed fusible web. Decorate a tree with one continuous garland or several shorter ones. Arrange the garland by weaving the ribbon between and into the branches to create depth.

HOW TO MAKE A ROPE GARLAND

MATERIALS

- 1⅓ yd. (1.27 m) two-ply or three-ply manila or sisal rope, ¼" or ⅜" (6 mm or 1 cm) in diameter.
- Sheet moss.
- Eight berry or floral clusters with wire stems, either purchased or made as on page 62.
- Wire cutter.
- Hot glue gun and glue sticks; thick craft glue.

1 Make 3" (7.5 cm) loops at ends of rope by inserting each end between plies; secure with hot glue.

2 Make eight berry or floral clusters, if necessary (page 62). Insert the wire stems of clusters between the plies of rope at 8" (20.5 cm) intervals, and secure them with hot glue; trim any excess wire, using wire cutter.

3 Conceal wire ends of clusters with pieces of sheet moss; secure with craft glue.

HOW TO MAKE A WRAPPED BALL-AND-SPOOL GARLAND

MATERIALS

- Scraps of cotton fabrics.
- Twenty-four ⅞" (2.2 cm) Styrofoam® balls.
- Twenty-four wooden craft spools.
- Assorted buttons, optional.
- Lightweight jute or twine.
- Large-eyed needle.
- Thick craft glue.

1 Tear twenty-four ¾" × 2¼" (2 × 6 cm) fabric strips on crosswise grain. Wrap around wooden spools; secure with glue. Tear twenty-four ½" × 13" (1.3 × 33 cm) fabric strips. Wrap randomly around Styrofoam balls; secure with glue.

2 Cut an 84" (213.5 cm) length of jute or twine. Form 3" (7.5 cm) loop at one end, and secure with knot; thread a large-eyed needle on opposite end.

3 String wrapped balls and spools onto jute or twine, alternating with buttons, if desired. Form loop at end; secure with knot.

HOW TO MAKE A DRIED-FRUIT-SLICE GARLAND

MATERIALS

- Firm apples and oranges.
- Fresh cranberries.
- Cinnamon sticks.
- 2 cups (500 mL) lemon juice.
- 1 tablespoon (15 mL) salt.
- Parchment paper.
- Raffia.
- 24-gauge floral wire.
- Wire cutter.
- Aerosol clear acrylic sealer.
- Paper towels.

1 Mix lemon and salt together; set aside. Cut fruit into scant ¼" (6 mm) slices, cutting crosswise as shown. Soak apple slices in lemon solution for 1 minute. Pat slices with paper towels to absorb excess moisture.

2 Place apple and orange slices on cookie sheet lined with parchment paper. Bake in 150°F (65°C) oven for 8 to 12 hours, until slices are dry, but still pliable; turn slices over and open oven door periodically while drying.

3 Apply aerosol clear acrylic sealer to cooled fruit slices. Break cinnamon sticks into 2" (5 cm) lengths. Select length of sturdy raffia; form loop at one end, and secure with knot.

4 Create needle for stringing fruit by folding a 6" (15 cm) length of floral wire in half around the unknotted end of raffia. Twist wire together at ends; trim excess, using wire cutter. Crimp the wire at fold, using pliers.

5 String the fruit slices, cranberries, and cinnamon sticks onto raffia; pierce fruit slices about ⅜" (1 cm) from the edges and gently ease along the raffia. Tie lengths of raffia together as necessary to make the garland about 72" (183 cm) long. Form a loop at end; secure with knot.

HOW TO MAKE A WIRED-RIBBON GARLAND

MATERIALS

- Fabric.
- One or more rolls of paper-backed fusible web, ⅜" (1 cm) wide.
- 26-gauge beading wire or craft wire.

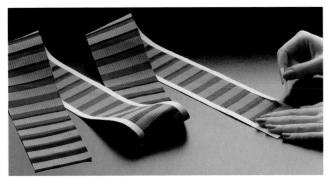

1 Cut fabric strips to desired width of ribbon plus ¾" (2 cm). Piece strips as necessary, as on page 52, step 7. Apply strip of fusible web to wrong side of fabric along both long edges, following the manufacturer's directions. Remove paper backing.

2 Cut wire slightly longer than the length of fabric. Place the wire along inner edge of one fused strip. Fold and press fused edge to wrong side of fabric, encasing wire. Repeat for opposite side. Trim wire at ends.

MORE IDEAS FOR GARLANDS

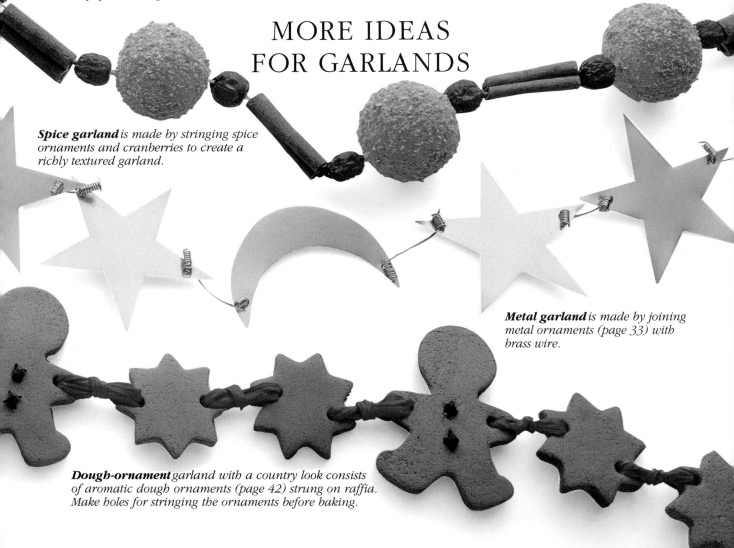

Spice garland is made by stringing spice ornaments and cranberries to create a richly textured garland.

Metal garland is made by joining metal ornaments (page 33) with brass wire.

Dough-ornament garland with a country look consists of aromatic dough ornaments (page 42) strung on raffia. Make holes for stringing the ornaments before baking.

QUICK & EASY GARLANDS

Candy canes and mint candies *are tied together with red ribbon for a colorful garland.*

Large bells *embellished with cones and sprigs of greenery are tied together with raffia.*

Holiday garlands are traditionally used to decorate the Christmas tree. Make your own garlands by securing items such as candies, cookie cutters, or floral materials together with ribbon, raffia, or fabric strips.

Mini cookie cutters in Christmas shapes are strung on lengths of jute. Beads are interspersed between the cookie cutters to add color to the garland.

Pretzels, tied to torn strips of fabric, make a country-style garland.

21

SCHERENSCHNITTE
ORNAMENTS & GARLANDS

Simple folding and cutting techniques turn ordinary paper into beautiful ornaments. The German craft of scherenschnitte (shear-en-shnit-tah), or scissors' cuttings, produces an intricate paper filigree that can be displayed as a single, flat ornament or a garland of repeated motifs. Single ornaments, glued to card stock, also make unique gift tags or Christmas cards. Two identical scherenschnitte pieces can be made and sewn together down the center for a three-dimensional ornament. Several patterns for each style are given on pages 152 to 156.

Ornaments can be antiqued, if desired, or tinted with watercolor paints or pastel chalks. For added sparkle, glitter may be applied to the ornament.

Choose art papers that have a sharp edge when cut. Parchment papers are particularly suitable for scherenschnitte, due to their strength and ability to accept stain or watercolors. Scissors with short, sharp, pointed blades are necessary for intricate work. Tiny detail cutting on the interior of the design is easier to do with a mat knife and cutting surface.

Three-dimensional ornament *is created by stitching two identical symmetrical designs together through the center. You can also make single ornaments or a garland as shown opposite.*

MATERIALS

- Tracing paper.
- Art paper.
- Graphite paper, for transferring design; removable tape; scrap of corrugated cardboard.
- Scissors with short, sharp, pointed blades.

- Mat knife and cutting surface.
- Needle; thread, for hanger.
- Instant coffee and cotton-tipped swab, for antiquing, optional.
- Watercolor paints, chalk pastels, and glitter, optional.

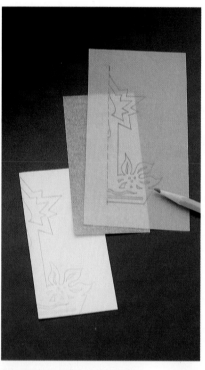

1 Cut a piece of art paper larger than the pattern dimensions (pages 152 to 156); for a symmetrical design, fold paper in half, right sides together. Trace pattern onto tracing paper. Transfer the design from tracing paper to wrong side of folded art paper, using graphite paper; align the dotted line on design to fold of art paper.

2 Tape folded art paper to cutting surface, placing the tape in area outside design. Cut out interior shapes, using mat knife; begin with shapes nearest fold, and work toward cut edges of paper. Make any small holes by punching through paper with a needle.

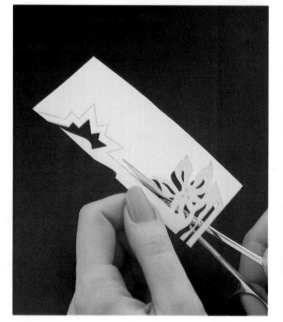

3 Remove art paper from cutting surface, and cut outer edge of design with scissors. Open cut design.

4 Press flat with a warm iron. Antique or embellish as desired, using one of the three methods on page 17. Attach thread hanger at center of the ornament, 1/4" (6 mm) from the upper edge, using a hand needle; knot the thread ends.

HOW TO MAKE A THREE-DIMENSIONAL
SCHERENSCHNITTE ORNAMENT

1 Follow steps 1 to 4, opposite, for two identical designs, omitting thread hanger. Place the cut designs on top of each other, aligning edges; secure to scrap of corrugated cardboard, using removable tape. Punch holes with pushpin every ¼" (6 mm) along the center fold, through both layers.

2 Thread a needle with 18" (46 cm) length of thread in same color as ornament. Sew in and out of holes from top to bottom of ornament.

3 Turn ornament over, and stitch back up to top hole. Tie the ends of thread together at desired length for hanger. Arrange the ornament sections at right angles to each other.

HOW TO MAKE A SCHERENSCHNITTE GARLAND

1 Cut strip of art paper 11" (28 cm) long and 2¾" (7 cm) wide. Fold in half, wrong sides together, to make 5½" × 4¼" (14 × 10.8 cm) strip. Fold short ends to center fold, right sides together, so the strip is accordion-folded, with wrong side facing out.

2 Trace design (page 156) for garland onto tracing paper. Transfer design from tracing paper to wrong side of folded art paper, using graphite paper; align dotted lines on design to double folded edges of paper.

3 Cut out the design, following steps 2 and 3 for single ornaments on page 24. Open out garland. Embellish, if desired, using one of the three methods opposite.

4 Repeat steps 1 to 3 as necessary to make as many garland lengths as desired. Press the garland pieces flat with a warm iron. Join garland lengths with small pieces of tape on wrong side.

Colored ornaments. Use watercolor paint or chalk pastels and soft brush to color scherenschnitte ornament. Allow to dry before painting an adjacent area. Press with warm iron, if desired. Repeat on back side.

Glittered ornaments. Apply glue over areas to be glittered, using glue pen. Sprinkle with glitter; shake off the excess. Repeat on back side.

Antiqued ornaments. Mix 1½ teaspoons (7 mL) instant coffee with ½ cup (125 mL) hot water. Apply coffee to outer edge of ornament and around large openings with cotton swab. Allow to dry; press. Repeat on back side.

HAND-CAST PAPER
ORNAMENTS

Though they may appear to be very delicate, these hand-cast paper ornaments are durable enough to become lasting keepsakes. Cotton linter is soaked in water and processed to a pulp, using a household blender. Paper-casting powder is added to the pulp for strength. Water is then strained from the mixture, and the pulp is pressed into a ceramic mold and allowed to dry.

After the ornament is removed from the mold, it may be painted, using water-color paints, or shaded, using chalk pastels. Tiny sprigs of dried floral material and narrow ribbons may be added for a Victorian look. For sparkle, fine glitter may be applied.

Supplies for making hand-cast paper ornaments are available at craft or art supply stores. They may be purchased separately or in kit form. One sheet of cotton linter measuring 8" × 7" (20.5 × 18 cm) will produce enough pulp for three hand-cast paper ornaments. The decorative ceramic molds have many other uses, making them a worthwhile purchase. Preparation of the mold before casting may vary with each brand; read manufacturer's instructions before beginning the project.

Leftover pulp can be saved for later use. Squeeze out excess water, and spread the pulp out in small clumps to dry. It is not necessary to add more paper-casting powder when resoaking and processing leftover pulp.

MATERIALS

- Cotton linter.
- Paper-casting powder, such as paper clay or paper additive.
- Household blender.
- Strainer.
- Ceramic casting mold.
- Sponge.
- Kitchen towel.
- Narrow ribbon or cord, for hanger; darning needle, for inserting hanger.
- Watercolor paints or chalk pastels, optional.
- Embellishments, such as dried floral materials, narrow ribbons, and glitter, optional.
- Craft glue, or hot glue gun and glue sticks, optional.

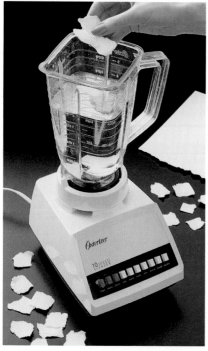

1 Tear 8" × 7" (20.5 × 18 cm) sheet of cotton linter into 1" (2.5 cm) pieces. Put in the blender with 1 quart (1 L) water; allow to soak for several minutes.

2 Blend the water and linter for 30 seconds on low speed. Add 1 teaspoon (5 mL) of paper-casting powder to mixture; blend on high speed for one minute.

3 Pour about one-third of mixture into strainer, draining off water. Put wet pulp into mold.

4 Spread pulp evenly around mold and out onto flat outer edges; pulp on flat edges will form deckled edge around border of ornament.

5 Press damp sponge over pulp, compressing it into the mold and drawing off excess water; wring out sponge. Repeat two or three times until excess water is removed.

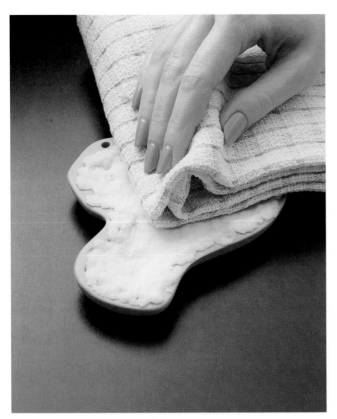

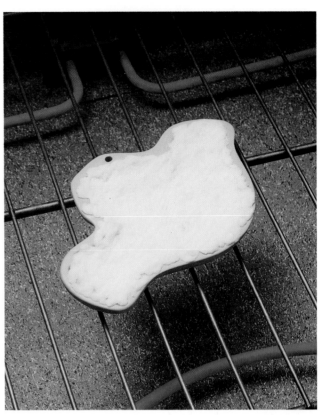

6 Press a folded kitchen towel over the compressed pulp, absorbing any remaining water and further compressing pulp.

7 Allow compressed pulp to dry completely in the mold. To speed drying, place the mold in an oven heated to 150°F (65°C) for about three hours.

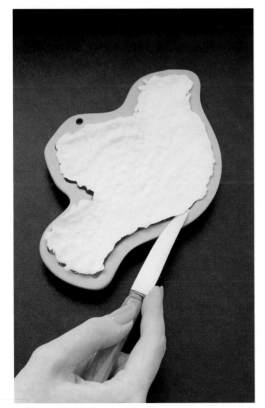

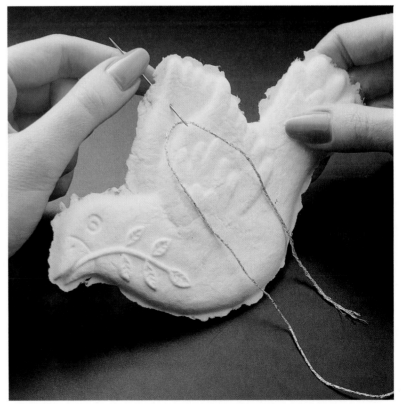

8 Loosen deckled edge of border around hand-cast paper ornament, using blade of knife; gently remove ornament from mold.

9 Thread cord or narrow ribbon into darning needle. Insert the needle through top of ornament at inner edge of border; knot ends of cord. Embellish ornament as desired (page 27).

METAL ORNAMENTS

Metal ornaments made from either copper or tin add a whimsical look to a tree. The metals are available at craft stores in sheets of various sizes. Copper is the thinner of the two and cuts easily with household utility scissors; tin can be cut best with a jeweler's snips, available at jewelry-making supply stores. Both metals are suitable for flat ornaments; however, tin can also be used to make spiral ornaments. To create chained ornaments, two or more ornaments can be wired together.

Metal ornaments can be embellished, if desired, with craft wire or a punched design. Simple shapes for the ornaments and the punched designs can be found on gift-wrapping paper, greeting cards, and cookie cutters.

You may enlarge or reduce simple designs on a photocopy machine, if desired.

For a country or rustic look, copper can easily be given a weathered or aged appearance through a process called oxidizing. Heat oxidizing is done by placing the copper ornament over a flame until the color changes. The copper ornament is moved randomly over the flame to produce uneven coloring. A gas stove works well for oxidizing copper, because it produces a clean flame. Hold the copper with tongs while heating, because the metal becomes very hot. For additional texture, sand the surface of the copper before it is heated, using medium-grit sandpaper.

MATERIALS

- Copper or tin sheet.
- Awl and rubber mallet, or tin-punching tool.
- Utility scissors or jeweler's snips.
- Scrap of wood.
- Tracing paper and transfer paper.
- Masking tape.

- 22-gauge to 28-gauge brass or copper craft wire.
- Fine steel wool.
- 100-grit sandpaper.
- Tongs with handles that do not conduct heat, for oxidizing copper.
- Aerosol clear acrylic sealer.

HOW TO MAKE A COPPER OR TIN FLAT ORNAMENT

1 Cover the work surface with a newspaper. Transfer the desired design for the ornament onto tracing paper. Transfer design to metal sheet, using transfer paper.

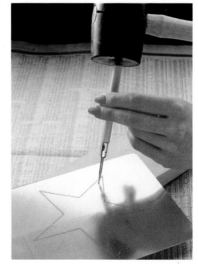

2 Place ornament design over scrap of wood. Punch hole for hanger about 1/8" (3 mm) inside edge of design, using an awl and mallet. Embellish interior of ornament with a punched design, if desired (page 35).

(Continued)

3 Cut out ornament, using scissors or jeweler's snips. Trim the tips off any sharp points.

4 Sand edges of ornament lightly, using sandpaper to smooth any sharp edges of metal; avoid sanding surface of ornament if smooth finish is desired.

5 Rub the ornament with fine steel wool to remove any fingerprints. Oxidize copper, if desired (opposite). Spray with aerosol clear acrylic sealer.

6 Embellish the ornament, if desired, by wrapping it with wire; for additional textural interest, layer two ornaments, then wrap with wire. Twist ends of wire together on back side; trim off excess.

7 Cut 7" (18 cm) length of wire, for hanger. Twist end of wire around awl, to make a coil, as in step 1, opposite. Insert opposite end of wire through the hole from the front of ornament; bend end to make hook for hanging.

HOW TO MAKE A TIN SPIRAL ORNAMENT

1 Cut ¼" × 6" (6 mm × 15 cm) strip of tin; trim ends at an angle. Trim off any sharp points, using jeweler's snips. Sand edges lightly with sandpaper. Punch a hole for hanger about ⅛" (3 mm) from one end of the strip, using an awl and mallet.

2 Wrap tin strip around pencil to make spiral; remove ornament from the pencil. Spray with aerosol clear acrylic sealer. Add hanger as in step 7, above.

HOW TO CONNECT METAL ORNAMENTS WITH WIRE

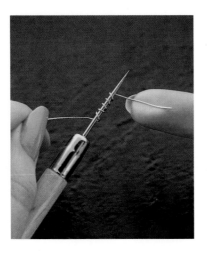

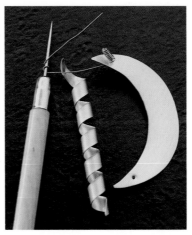

1 Cut 6" (15 cm) length of wire. Twist end of wire around awl to make a coil, using about 2¼" (6 cm) of wire. Press coil together between fingers to compress slightly.

2 Insert opposite end of the wire through hole in one ornament from front. Insert wire through second ornament from back. Repeat coiling process to secure the wire to second ornament.

HOW TO PUNCH A DESIGN IN A METAL ORNAMENT

1 Transfer the design for punching to tissue paper as on page 33, step 1. Tape the design for punching to metal sheet inside lines for ornament.

2 Punch holes around the edges of design at ⅛" (3 mm) intervals, using awl and mallet. Remove tissue pattern.

HOW TO OXIDIZE COPPER

1 Texturize copper sheet, if desired, by sanding lightly with sandpaper.

2 Hold the copper ornament over flame with tongs; move it through flame randomly to produce color change. Remove the ornament from heat occasionally to check for desired color; holding the copper in flame too long can cause the copper to lose all its natural color.

PAPIER-MÂCHÉ ORNAMENTS

Create easy-to-make papier-mâché ornaments from ready-made forms, available at craft shops. Simply embellish the forms with a variety of paints, beads, or glitter for a shimmering holiday display.

TIPS FOR EMBELLISHING PAPIER-MÂCHÉ ORNAMENTS

Paint the ornaments with aerosol acrylic paint; use pearlescent paint for a lustrous finish.

Apply glitter glue to painted ornaments to create a shimmering raised design.

Embellish the ornaments with beads; secure with craft glue.

GOLD-LEAF ORNAMENTS

Turn papier-mâché craft ornaments into elegant gold-leaf ornaments, using imitation gold leaf.

Imitation leaf, also available in silver and copper, can be found at craft and art supply stores. Several sheets are packaged together, with tissue paper between the layers. When working with the sheets of gold leaf, handle the tissue paper, not the gold leaf, whenever possible. The gold leaf is very fragile and may tarnish.

MATERIALS

- Papier-mâché ball.
- Aerosol acrylic paint, optional.
- Imitation gold, silver, or copper leaf.
- Gold-leaf adhesive; paintbrush.
- Soft-bristle brush.
- Ribbon, for bow.
- Thick craft glue; aerosol clear acrylic sealer.

HOW TO MAKE A GOLD-LEAF ORNAMENT

1 Apply aerosol paint to the papier-mâché ball, if desired; allow paint to dry. Apply gold-leaf adhesive to the ornament in small area, feathering out edges; allow the adhesive to dry until clear.

2 Cut the gold leaf and tissue paper slightly larger than adhesive area. Press the gold leaf over the adhesive, handling the tissue only. Remove the tissue paper.

3 Remove excess gold leaf with a soft-bristle brush. Apply gold leaf to additional areas of ball as desired. Apply aerosol clear acrylic sealer. Tie ribbon in bow around base of hanger; secure with dot of craft glue.

MARBLEIZED ORNAMENTS

Elegant marbleized ornaments are easy to make, using clear glass ornaments and craft acrylic paints. For best results, use paints that are of pouring consistency; paints may be thinned with water, if necessary. The marbleized effect is created by pouring two or three colors of paint into a glass ornament and swirling the paint colors together. Allow the paints to dry slightly after each color is applied, to avoid a muddy appearance.

MATERIALS

- Clear glass ornament, with removable top.
- Craft acrylic paints in desired colors.
- 9" (23 cm) length of cording or ribbon, for hanger.
- Ribbon, for bow.
- Disposable cups; hot glue gun and glue sticks.

HOW TO MAKE A MARBLEIZED ORNAMENT

1 Remove cap from ornament. Pour first color of paint into disposable cup; thin with water, if necessary. Pour small amount of paint into ornament; rotate to swirl paint. Place ornament, upside down, on the cup; allow any excess paint to flow out.

2 Repeat step 1 for each remaining color of paint. Place the ornament, upside down, on a cup, and allow the excess paint to flow out. Turn ornament right side up; allow to dry. Paint colors will continue to mix together during the drying process. Use additional coats of paint as necessary for opaque appearance.

3 Replace cap on ornament. Insert cording or ribbon through wire loop in cap; knot ends. Make a bow from ribbon; secure to top of ornament, using hot glue.

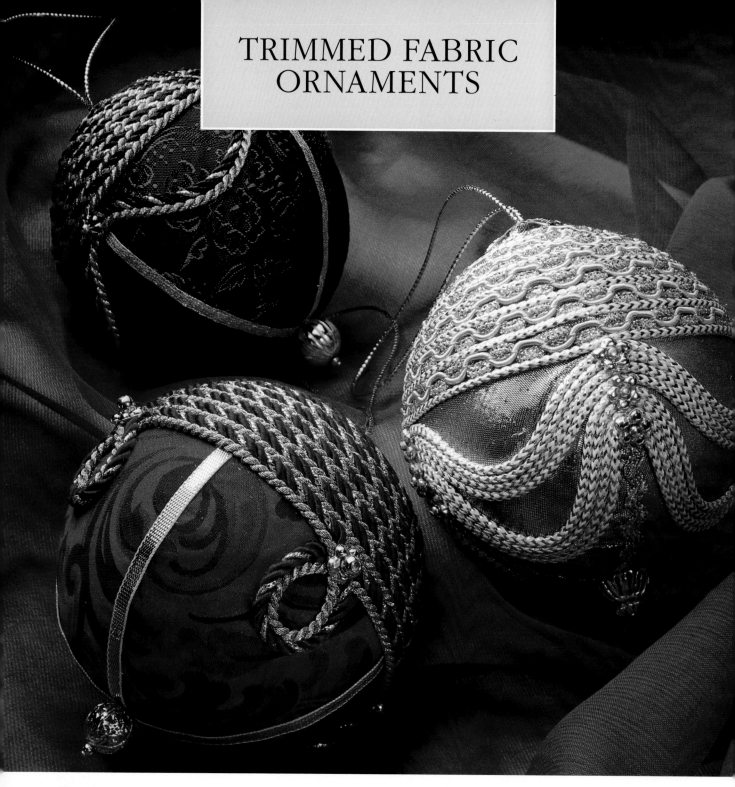

TRIMMED FABRIC ORNAMENTS

$\mathbf{C}$reate elegant ornaments by covering Styrofoam® balls with rich fabrics and trims. Four wedge-shaped fabric pieces are used to cover the Styrofoam ball. Use one fabric, or select up to four different coordinating fabrics, to cover the ball. The fabric pieces are glued to the ball, and the raw edges are concealed with flat trim, such as ribbon or braid. Cording, pearls, sequins, or beads can also be used to embellish the ornament. The hanger of the ornament is made from a decorative cord and an ornamental cap.

MATERIALS

- 3" (7.5 cm) Styrofoam ball.
- Fabric scraps.
- Cording and flat trims, such as ribbon or braid.
- Decorative beads, pearls, sequins, and bead pins, optional.
- 9" (23 cm) length of cording and ornamental cap, for hanger.
- Thick craft glue; hot glue gun and glue sticks.

HOW TO MAKE A TRIMMED FABRIC ORNAMENT

1 Transfer the pattern (page 154) to paper, and cut four pieces from fabric scraps.

2 Apply craft glue near the edges on the wrong side of one fabric piece. Position the fabric piece on Styrofoam ball; smooth edges around the ball, easing fullness along sides.

3 Apply remaining fabric pieces to ball; match points and align raw edges to cover ball completely.

4 Glue trim over the raw edges of the fabric pieces, butting raw edges of trim at top of ornament.

5 Poke hole in Styrofoam ball at top of ornament. Insert end of one or two pieces of cording into hole; secure with craft glue. Apply glue to fabric as shown; wrap the cording tightly around the ball in one continuous spiral, until desired effect is achieved. Poke end of cording into Styrofoam; secure with glue.

6 Embellish with additional cording, if desired. Attach decorative beads, pearls, and sequins, if desired, using bead pins; secure with dot of craft glue.

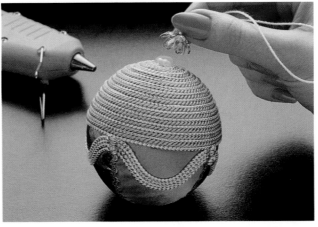

7 Insert cord in decorative cap; knot ends. Shape cap to fit top of ornament; secure with hot glue. Add bead or decorative cap to bottom, if desired.

AROMATIC DOUGH ORNAMENTS

For an old-fashioned country look, you can decorate the Christmas tree with aromatic dough ornaments. A variety of ornaments can be created, depending on the shapes of cookie cutters used. Either a microwave or a conventional oven can be used for making the ornaments. The conventional oven method may produce ornaments with a more irregular surface. The microwave directions are based on a 600-watt microwave oven. The cooking time and finished product may vary, depending on the wattage and size of your microwave oven.

For added embellishment, decorate the ornaments with whole cloves, allspice, cinnamon candies, or bits of dough. Hang the ornaments from the tree with ribbon, raffia, or torn strips of cotton fabric.

MATERIALS

- Ingredients for aromatic dough, opposite.
- Mixing bowl; floured board; rolling pin; cookie cutters.
- 10" (25.5 cm) pie plate for microwave method, or baking sheet for conventional oven method.
- Garlic press, optional.
- Drinking straw, ⅜" (1 cm) in diameter.
- Nonstick vegetable cooking spray.
- 9" (23 cm) length of ribbon or raffia, for hanger.
- Embellishments, such as cinnamon candies, whole cloves, or allspice.

AROMATIC DOUGH

2¾ cups (675 mL) all-purpose flour

¾ cup (175 mL) salt

¼ cup (50 mL) ground cinnamon

1 tablespoon (15 mL) ground allspice

1 tablespoon (15 mL) ground cloves

¾ teaspoon (4 mL) powdered alum

1¼ cups (300 mL) water

Combine flour, salt, cinnamon, allspice, cloves, and alum in a medium mixing bowl. Add water. Mix well to form dough. Shape the dough into ball. Knead on lightly floured board for about 5 minutes, or until dough is smooth. (If too stiff, sprinkle with additional water; if too moist, add flour.) Spray pie plate or baking sheet with nonstick vegetable cooking spray; set aside. For conventional oven method, heat oven to 250°F (120°C).

1 Prepare aromatic dough (left). Roll dough to ¼" (6 mm) thickness on lightly floured surface; work with small portions of the dough at a time. Cut out the shapes with cookie cutters.

2 Embellish cutouts with cinnamon candies, cloves, allspice, or bits of textured dough; make the textured dough by pushing small amounts of dough through a garlic press. Secure the dough to cutouts by moistening it with water. Cut hole for hanger near top of cutout, using drinking straw.

3 Spray pie plate or baking sheet with vegetable cooking spray. Place cutouts on prepared pie plate or baking sheet. Microwave or bake in conventional oven as directed below. **Microwave oven method.** Cook at 30% (Medium Low) for 5 to 8 minutes, or until the tops of the cutouts feel dry, rotating the plate and checking the ornaments every 2 minutes. **Conventional oven method.** Bake for about 2 hours, or until tops are dry and feel firm to the touch.

4 Remove ornaments to a rack and set aside for 24 hours or longer to complete drying. If desired, spray the ornaments lightly with vegetable cooking spray for glossier appearance. Insert the ribbon or raffia for hangers through the holes of the ornaments; knot ends together.

Note: *These ornaments are for decoration only.*

QUICK & EASY ORNAMENTS

Wheat bundles (left), hung upside down, are attractive accents on trees with natural or country decorating styles. The wheat stems are secured in bundles with a rubber band, which is concealed with a fabric bow. Secure the ornaments to the tree using floral wire.

Wire garland, shaped into spirals, adds glitz to a Christmas tree. Wrap a 26" (66 cm) length of wire garland around a pen or pencil. Remove the wire, then gradually untwist the coil from one end to make the ornament. At the widest end, bend the wire to form a hanger.

Glitter adds sparkle to plain ornaments. Mark designs on the ornaments using a glue-stick pen, then sprinkle with extra-fine glitter.

Dried fruit slices make aromatic ornaments. Orange slices, glued together, are decorated with sprigs of greenery, berries, and ribbon hangers. The apple slices have jute hangers and are embellished with anise and cinnamon sticks. Dried fruit slices are available at craft stores, or make your own as on pages 16 and 18.

Torn fabric strips are wrapped and glued around Styrofoam® balls to make country-style ornaments. Secure raffia bows and hangers with hot glue.

Ribbons and berries embellish the tops of purchased glass ornaments. Ribbons also replace the traditional wire hangers.

Glitter glue in fine-tip tubes is applied to a glass ball ornament, creating a unique dimensional design.

LAYERED TREE SKIRTS

Decorate the base of a Christmas tree with a layered tree skirt embellished with ribbon bows. When arranged around the tree, it resembles an eight-pointed star. The skirt can be made for either an elegant or casual look, depending on the choice of fabrics and ribbon.

Easy to make, the tree skirt is simply two lined squares of fabric, stitched together around center openings. Back openings in the layers allow for easy placement around the tree. Safety pins, used in place of permanent stitching, gather the fabric along each side, saving time and allowing the tree skirt to be stored flat.

Choose a lightweight lining fabric to prevent adding bulk to the skirt. For an inexpensive lining that is also a good choice for sheer fabrics, use nylon net.

Layered tree skirt is *made from printed and plaid complementary holiday fabrics. Solid-colored fabrics are used for the lining. The tree skirt is embellished with wired ribbon bows.*

MATERIALS

- 1¼ yd. (1.15 m) each, of two coordinating fabrics.
- 1¼ yd. (1.15 m) each, of two lining fabrics.
- Eight large safety pins.
- Wired ribbon.

HOW TO MAKE A LAYERED TREE SKIRT

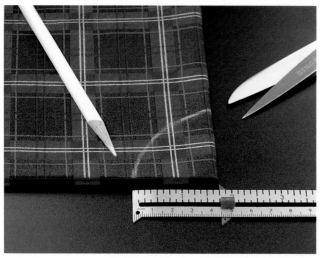

1 Cut outer fabric into a square, trimming selvages. Fold fabric in half lengthwise, then crosswise. Mark an arc, measuring 1¾" (4.5 cm) from folded center of fabric. Cut on marked line.

2 Pin-mark one folded edge at raw edges for the center back opening; open fabric and mark cutting line from raw edge to center opening, on wrong side of fabric.

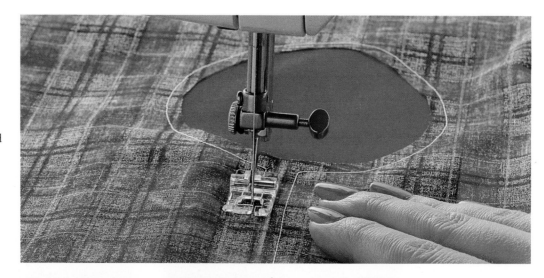

3 Place face fabric on lining, right sides together; pin the layers together. Stitch ¼" (6 mm) seam around tree skirt, stitching around all edges and on each side of center back line; leave 6" (15 cm) opening for turning. For sheer fabrics, stitch a second row scant ⅛" (3 mm) from first stitching.

4 Cut on marked line; trim lining even with edges of outer fabric. Clip seam allowances around center circle; trim corners diagonally. Turn right side out; press. Slipstitch opening closed.

5 Repeat steps 1 to 4 for the remaining tree skirt layer. Align skirts, right sides up, matching center back openings. Shift the upper skirt so corners of the lower skirt are centered at sides of upper skirt. Mark opening of lower skirt on upper skirt. Pin layers together around the center from marked point to opening in the upper skirt.

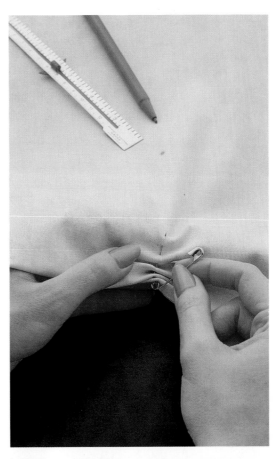

6 Topstitch ¼" (6 mm) from the raw edges around center, from opening to marked point, securing the two tree skirt layers together.

7 Gather and bunch fabric at the center of one long edge by inserting point of safety pin in and out of fabric for about 6" (15 cm) on lining side of the tree skirt as shown; close the pin. Repeat at center of each side for each tree skirt layer; do not pin back opening sides.

8 Place skirt around base of tree. Overlap back opening at outer edge; gather and bunch fabric for underlayer with safety pin. Repeat for remaining center back opening of upper layer of skirt.

9 Make four ribbon bows. Position a bow at each side of the upper layer, concealing safety pin; secure with pin.

TREE SKIRTS

A tree skirt offers the finishing touch to a Christmas tree. This simple lined tree skirt, finished with bias binding, has a layer of polyester fleece or batting for added body. It can be embellished in a variety of ways, using fused appliqués.

Make the patterns for appliqué designs by enlarging simple motifs found on Christmas cards or gift-wrapping paper. Use machine quilting or hand stitching around the outer edges of the appliqués to give them more definition.

MATERIALS

- 1¼ yd. (1.15 m) fabric, for tree skirt.
- 1¼ yd. (1.15 m) lining fabric.
- 45" (115 cm) square polyester fleece or low-loft quilt batting.
- ¾ yd. (0.7 m) fabric, for binding.
- Scraps of fabric, for fused appliqués.
- Paper-backed fusible web.

CUTTING DIRECTIONS

Cut the fabric, lining, and fleece or batting as in steps 1 to 3, below. Cut bias fabric strips, 2½" (6.5 cm) wide, for the binding.

HOW TO SEW A BIAS-BOUND TREE SKIRT

1 Fold fabric for tree skirt in half lengthwise, then crosswise. Using a straightedge and a pencil, mark an arc on the fabric, measuring 21" to 22" (53.5 to 56 cm) from folded center of fabric. Cut on the marked line through all layers.

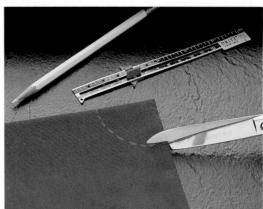

2 Mark a second arc, measuring 1¾" (4.5 cm) from the folded center of the fabric. Cut on the marked line.

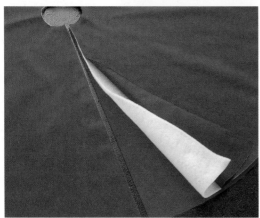

3 Cut along one folded edge; this will be the center back. Cut lining and fleece or batting, using fabric for tree skirt as a pattern.

4 Apply the paper-backed fusible web to the wrong side of fabric scraps, following the manufacturer's directions. Transfer design motifs onto paper side of the fusible web; turn pattern over if the design is asymmetrical.

(Continued)

5 Cut design motifs from paper-backed fabric; remove paper backing. Fuse motifs to the tree skirt as desired.

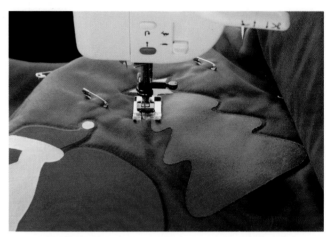

6 Layer the lining, fleece, and fabric for tree skirt, right sides out. Baste the layers together, using safety pins or hand stitching. Quilt design motifs by stitching around the outer edges of designs.

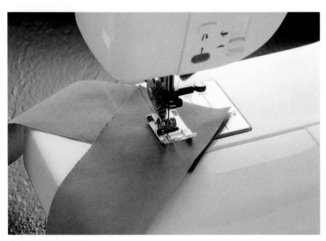

7 Piece binding strips to form 5½-yd. (5.05 m) length; join the strips together as shown; trim ¼" (6 mm) from stitching. Press seams open; trim off points.

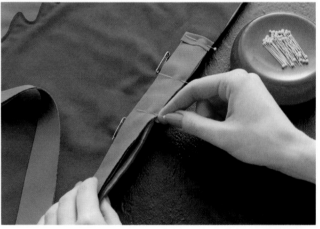

8 Press the binding strip in half lengthwise, wrong sides together; fold back ½" (1.3 cm) on one short end. Pin binding to tree skirt, matching raw edges and starting at center back.

9 Stitch a scant ⅜" (1 cm) from raw edges, overlapping ends of binding ½" (1.3 cm); trim close to stitching.

10 Wrap binding strip snugly around edge of tree skirt, covering the stitching line on the wrong side; pin. Stitch in the ditch on right side of tree skirt, catching the binding on the wrong side.

MORE IDEAS FOR TREE SKIRTS

Gingerbread-men appliqués embellish this tree skirt. The outer edge is defined with contrasting bias binding and jumbo rickrack. The rickrack is applied to the underside of the tree skirt after the binding is applied. The gingerbread men are embellished with fabric paints in fine-tip tubes.

Star-and-moon theme is created using appliqués from lamé fabric. To prevent the delicate fabric from fraying, the raw edges of the appliqués were sealed, using fabric paints in fine-tip tubes.

Bullion fringe adds an elegant edging to a brocade tree skirt. Applied to the underside of the tree skirt, the fringe is secured in place by edgestitching along the inside edge of the binding from the right side.

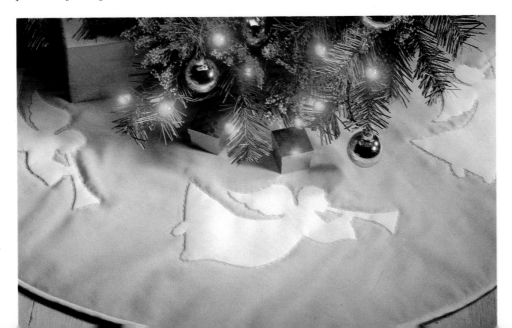

Sheer organza overlay, placed over the fused angel appliqués, creates a shadow embroidery effect. The tree skirt is quilted around the outer edges of the appliqués, using two strands of embroidery thread and a hand running stitch.

MORE IDEAS FOR TREE SKIRTS

Polar fleece tree skirt *(above), with fringed edges, requires minimal sewing. To make the round skirt, mark arcs for the outer edge and the center opening as on page 50, steps 1 and 2. Apply the appliqués by hand with a decorative blanket stitch, or by machine with topstitching. Cut the fringe, keeping the blade of the scissors perpendicular to the edge of the fabric.*

Lace tablecloth, *draped around the base of a tree, complements a Victorian-style tree.*

Excelsior, *highlighted with gold spray paint, is arranged around the base of a Christmas tree for a unique accent.*

Around The House

DECORATING MANTELS

Family photographs *from previous Christmases are grouped on a mantel for a nostalgic look. Honeysuckle vine and dried hydrangeas are used to embellish the artificial garland.*

Mantels are the perfect place to showcase Christmas decorations. Evergreen boughs or garlands displayed on a mantel can serve as a backdrop for a collection of family photos, Santas, unique ornaments, or hand-crafted Christmas items. For interest, mix a few dried or artificial floral elements with traditional Christmas accessories.

Safety note: Do not leave any open flame, including candles, unattended.

Gilded reindeer
and candles in brass
candlesticks (above)
are arranged on an
ornate mantel with
greenery, cones,
and berries. The
papier-mâché
reindeer were gilded
with metallic paint.

Amaryllis (right)
are set on each
side of a picture,
dominating this
Christmas display.

Countdown calender (below) is made by hanging twenty-four tea-dyed stocking ornaments, filled with holiday candies,
along a fresh garland. A star ornament hangs at the end of the garland for Christmas Day.

EMBELLISHING WREATHS

Honeysuckle vine *encircles an artificial wreath. A gilded reindeer and gold bow are elegant highlights. Artichokes, cones, hydrangea, and pomegranates add textural interest.*

Wreaths can be embellished for a variety of looks. For the base, select a fresh or artificial evergreen wreath, or a grapevine wreath. Embellish the base with items such as ribbons, ornaments, and floral materials to create a wreath that reflects your personal style.

Artificial evergreen wreaths are especially easy to decorate, because many items can be secured by simply twisting the branches around the embellishments. Items can also be secured to wreaths using floral wire or hot glue.

Embellish wreaths with one material at a time, spacing the items evenly to achieve a balanced look. Add large items first and fill in any bare areas with smaller ones. Secure embellishments to the surface as well as to the wreath base, to give a sense of depth.

Artificial evergreen garland is wrapped around a grapevine wreath. A natural look is created by adding birch bark and twig birdhouses, artificial birds, and stems of rose hips.

Santa's elf (page 92) is wired to the center area of this fresh wreath to create a focal point. Dried fruit slices, cinnamon sticks, and paper twist are added to give this wreath a country look.

Wire-mesh bow (page 11) and metal ornaments (page 33) are used to embellish a fresh evergreen wreath. The mesh strips for the bow measure about 4" (10 cm) wide and 24" (61 cm) long. Lights were added to the wreath before it was decorated.

Village house becomes the focal point of an artificial · wreath. Additional sprigs of greenery, cones, and berries are added for texture and fullness. For a snowy effect, aerosol artificial snow is sprayed over polyester fiberfill.

TIPS FOR EMBELLISHING WREATHS

Attach wire to a cone by wrapping the wire around bottom layers of cone. Attach wire to a cinnamon stick by inserting it through length of stick; wrap wire around stick, and twist the ends at the middle.

Make floral or berry clusters by grouping items together. Attach wire to the items as necessary. Wrap stems and wires with floral tape.

Add texture to a wreath by inserting sprigs of other evergreen varieties. Secure sprigs to the wreath base, using wire.

Display Christmas collectibles, such as village houses and ornaments, on a wreath for visual impact. Wire items securely to the wreath base.

Gild embellishments, such as twigs, cones, artichokes, and sprigs of greenery, by applying gold aerosol acrylic paint.

Embellish wreath with ribbon by weaving it through the wreath; create twists and turns for depth. Secure the ribbon as necessary with hot glue.

Wrap honeysuckle vine loosely over a wreath, for added texture. Secure the vine with floral wire or hot glue.

Wrap artificial garland around a grapevine wreath to add color and dimension.

Add battery-operated lights to a wreath by weaving the cords into the wreath boughs.

Embellish bows with additional loops of contrasting ribbon. Fold length of ribbon in half to form loop the same size as loops on the existing bow; wrap ends tightly with wire. Secure to the center of bow, using hot glue.

TOPIARY TREES

Make a classic topiary tree to accent your fireplace or display on a sideboard for the holidays. This finished tree measures about 24" (61 cm) tall. Embellish the top of this miniature tree with artificial fruit, floral materials, and decorative ribbon. The tree is set in a terra-cotta pot.

MATERIALS

- 4" (10 cm) Styrofoam® ball.
- Artificial pine boughs.
- Wired ribbon.
- Latex grape clusters and small pears.
- Dried yarrow.
- Small red-leaf preserved foliage; artificial green leaves.
- 7" (18 cm) terra-cotta pot.
- Floral foam, for silk arranging.
- Several dogwood stems.
- Hot glue gun and glue sticks.

1 Trim floral foam with a knife to fit pot snugly; secure with hot glue. Cut dogwood stems about 14" (35.5 cm) long. Insert several stems into center of the pot; secure with hot glue.

HOW TO MAKE A TOPIARY TREE

(Continued)

65

2 Secure the opposite ends of the stems to one side of the Styrofoam® ball, using hot glue.

3 Cut pine boughs into pieces about 3" (7.5 cm) long. Insert the pine stems into ball and foam in pot until the surfaces are covered.

4 Cut apart the grape stems and pears; insert as desired, securing with hot glue. Insert a large grape cluster into pot, allowing it to cascade over edge.

5 Cut red-leaf foliage into 4" (10 cm) stems. Secure leaf stems and yarrow pieces to ball with hot glue. Tuck the ribbon into ball; secure with hot glue, if necessary.

WALL TREES

Make a stunning wall accent from a miniature artificial pine tree. The branches of the tree are bent to the front, creating a flat surface in the back. This allows the tree to be displayed flat against a wall. The wall tree is embellished with a variety of fruit and is topped with a large bow.

MATERIALS

- Artificial pine tree with attached trunk, about 24" (61 cm) tall.
- Four or five varieties of fruit, including apples, pears, grape clusters, and berries.
- Preserved leaves on stems.
- 3 yd. (2.75 m) wired ribbon, for bow.
- Floral wire.

1 Bend branches of artificial tree around to one side. Place flat on table, and arrange branches.

2 Secure pears to tree with hot glue, forming a curved diagonal line as shown.

3 Gild leaves as on page 71, step 1. Secure thin layer of gilded leaves along sides of pears, using hot glue. Lift pine boughs to surround the row of pears and leaves. Insert second variety of fruit and another row of gilded leaves, following the same line as the pears; secure with hot glue.

4 Continue to secure alternating rows of fruit and gilded leaves, until the entire tree is covered. Arrange pine boughs between rows of fruit and leaves.

5 Form large loops from wired ribbon as shown **(a).** Continue to make six loops. Make small loop at center. Bend wire around ribbon at center; twist wire tightly, gathering ribbon **(b).** Separate and shape the loops.

6 Secure bow to top of tree, using wire. Twist excess wire into loop at back, for hanging tree. Tuck ends of ribbon into sides of tree.

HOLIDAY FLORAL ARRANGEMENTS

Use this unique floral arrangement to add color to your holiday table. Make the arrangement from the floral materials shown, or select floral materials to coordinate with your decorating scheme.

To help create the elegant natural look of the arrangement, the preserved leaves are highlighted with gold paint. Try this simple highlighting technique on other floral materials to achieve interesting effects. The gold highlights complement the gilded terra-cotta pots that are used for the base of the arrangement.

MATERIALS

- Two terra-cotta pots, about 5" (12.5 cm) in diameter.
- Gold aerosol paint, plus optional second color.
- Floral foam, for silk arranging.
- Artificial pine boughs.
- Latex grape clusters and apples; dried pomegranates.
- 3 yd. (2.75 m) stiff decorative cording.
- Artificial or preserved leaves on branches; twigs.
- Hot glue gun and glue sticks.

HOW TO MAKE A HOLIDAY FLORAL ARRANGEMENT

1 Place a sheet of plastic on a tabletop. Spray a generous pool of aerosol paint onto the plastic; drag the preserved leaves through the paint to gild them. Allow to dry. Repeat with additional paint colors, if desired.

2 Place one pot on its side, next to the other; secure pots together, using hot glue. When dry, apply gold aerosol paint to the containers.

(Continued)

71

3 Cut floral foam, using knife, so it fits container snugly and is even with edge of container; secure with hot glue. Repeat for remaining container.

4 Insert pine boughs and leaf branches into foam, so they rise from 5" to 8" (12.5 to 20.5 cm) above foam. Cut pine branches into small pieces to fill area around edges of containers. Insert a few twigs into vertical pot.

5 Insert apples and grape clusters, allowing some of the grapes to cascade slightly over sides of containers. Secure pomegranates into arrangement as desired with hot glue.

6 Apply tape to decorative braid at 8" to 12" (20.5 to 30.5 cm) intervals; cut braid through center of tape. Form loops from lengths of braid; wrap ends together with tape. Insert loops of decorative braid into arrangement, securing braid to foam with hot glue.

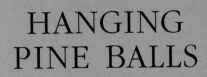

A holiday pine ball is created by decorating a Styrofoam® ball with pine stems, preserved leaves, and artificial berries. Display the pine ball indoors by hanging it from either a window or door frame, using a decorative ribbon and an upholstery tack. The pine ball can also be hung outdoors, offering a festive welcome to holiday guests.

MATERIALS

- 4" (10 cm) Styrofoam ball.
- Artificial pine boughs.
- Small-leaf preserved foliage.
- Artificial berries.
- Ribbon; floral wire.

HOW TO MAKE A HANGING PINE BALL

1 Cut several pieces of pine into 1½" (3.8 cm) lengths. Insert pine lengths into ball until surface is covered. Insert short pieces of small-leaf foliage into the ball, interspersing them among pine lengths. Cut sprigs of berries, and insert berries as desired.

2 Make six ribbon loops; secure with glue at center as shown. Cut ribbon to desired length for hanger. Cut 8" (20.5 cm) length of wire. Hold end of ribbon over wire; secure with glue. Bend wire ends down; insert wire ends into the foam ball over ribbon loops.

FRESH FLORAL ARRANGEMENTS

Decorate for the holidays with fresh flowers by making a centerpiece or a buffet arrangement. A centerpiece used on a dining table is usually short in height so it does not interfere with conversation. A buffet arrangement is designed to be placed against a wall and can be taller, for more impact.

To make a holiday arrangement, use long-lasting flowers such as those on page 76 and add sprigs of greenery, such as Scotch pine, spruce, or juniper. For a more festive look, embellish the arrangement with canella berries, decorative pods, pepper berries, pinecones, feathers, or seeded eucalyptus.

A fresh holiday arrangement can be displayed in any container that holds water. For baskets, terra-cotta pots, or metal pots, use a plastic waterproof container as a liner.

Fresh flowers can be held in the arrangement by either of two methods, depending on the container selected. For glass containers, the flowers are held in place by making a grid over the mouth of the container with clear waterproof tape. For nonglass containers, the flowers are held in place by inserting them into floral foam designed for fresh flowers.

MATERIALS

- Flowers in three sizes.
- Sprigs of two or more varieties of greenery.
- Tall linear floral material, such as gilded devil's claw heliconia, curly willow, or branches, for the buffet arrangement.
- Gilded pods, berries, or twigs, for the centerpiece.
- Floral foam, designed for fresh flowers, for use with nonglass containers.
- Clear waterproof floral tape.
- Sharp knife.

TIPS FOR FRESH FLOWERS

Cut off 1" (2.5 cm) from stems, at an angle, before arranging; for roses, cut stems at an angle while submerging them in water.

Remove any leaves that will be covered by water in the finished arrangement; leaves left in the water will shorten the life of the flowers.

Add cut-flower food to the water.

Add fresh water to the floral arrangement as necessary.

Keep flowers out of direct sunlight and drafts.

Centerpiece (above) combines chrysanthemums, roses, ornithogalum, leatherleaf, seeded eucalyptus, lotus pods, and cedar. Buffet arrangement (opposite) uses mums, lilies, leptosporum, roses, gilded devil's claw heliconia, leatherleaf, and seeded eucalyptus to create a dramatic display.

Chrysanthemums

Ornithogalum

Heather

Lily

Carnations

Orchid

Yarrow

Roses

Alstroemeria

Stock

Leptosporum

Flowers shown above can be used to make long-lasting holiday arrangements.

HOW TO PREPARE THE CONTAINER

1 **Nonglass containers.** Soak the floral foam in water for at least 20 minutes.

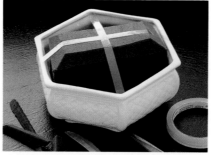

2 Cut foam, using a knife, so it fits the container and extends about 1" (2.5 cm) above rim. Round off the upper edges of foam, if necessary, to prevent foam from showing in the finished arrangement. Secure with clear waterproof tape. Add water.

Glass containers. Make a grid over the mouth of container, using clear waterproof floral tape.

HOW TO MAKE A FRESH FLORAL BUFFET ARRANGEMENT

1 Prepare glass or nonglass container (above). Insert first variety of greenery into container, placing taller stems into center near back and shorter stems at sides and front.

2 Insert remaining varieties of greenery. Insert tall linear materials into container, spacing them evenly.

76

3 Insert largest flowers into the arrangement, one variety at a time, spacing them evenly throughout to keep arrangement balanced on three sides.

4 Insert second largest flowers into arrangement, spacing evenly. Insert the smaller flowers into the arrangement to fill any bare areas. Mist arrangement lightly with water.

HOW TO MAKE A FRESH FLORAL CENTERPIECE

1 Prepare the glass or nonglass container (opposite). Cut sprigs of greenery to lengths of 5" to 8" (12.5 to 20.5 cm); trim away any stems near the ends of sprigs.

2 Insert sprigs of greenery into the container, placing longer sprigs around the outside and shorter sprigs near the center.

3 Insert the largest flowers into the container, placing one stem in the center and several stems on each side to establish the height and width of the arrangement. Insert remaining large flowers, spacing evenly.

4 Insert the second largest flowers into the arrangement, one variety at a time, spacing evenly, so the arrangement appears balanced from all sides.

5 Insert additional sprigs of greenery as necessary to fill in any bare areas. Insert gilded pods, twigs, or berries, if desired, for further embellishment. Mist arrangement lightly with water.

JEWELED TREE

Make an elegant jeweled tree to accent a holiday table or buffet. Or group several trees of various sizes together to create a mantel display. Simple to make, the jeweled tree is constructed by wrapping beaded garland and decorative cording around a Styrofoam® cone. The jeweled tree can be further embellished with miniature ornaments or topped with a larger ornament.

To assemble the tree, the Styrofoam cone is mounted on a painted dowel and set in a container of plaster of Paris. To conceal the container, wrap it with a fabric circle, tied with decorative cording.

MATERIALS

- Styrofoam cone in desired size up to 15" (38 cm).
- Paper twist.
- One or two beaded garlands.
- Decorative cording.
- Wooden Shaker box, 4½" (11.5 cm) in diameter.
- Dowel, ⅝" (1.5 cm) in diameter.
- Aerosol acrylic paint in color that blends with colors of beaded garland and decorative cording, optional.
- ½ yd. (0.5 m) fabric, for base.
- ½ yd. (0.5 m) lining fabric, for base, if contrasting lining is desired.
- ½ yd. (0.5 m) decorative cording, for base.
- Plaster of Paris.
- Rubber band.
- Hot glue gun and glue sticks.
- Miniature ornaments or embellishments, optional.

CUTTING DIRECTIONS

Cut one 17" (43 cm) circle from the fabric and the lining, for the base. Cut a 1½" (3.8 cm) slit in the center of the lining circle.

HOW TO MAKE A JEWELED TREE

1 Line Shaker box with two layers of aluminum foil. Crumple the foil loosely to shape of the box, to allow room for the plaster to expand as it dries; edge of the foil should be ¼" (6 mm) below top of box.

2 Insert trunk of tree into cone to one-third the height of the cone. Place trunk in box, and adjust height of tree by cutting trunk to the desired length. Remove cone from trunk.

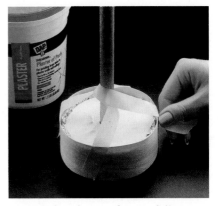

3 Mix the plaster of Paris, following manufacturer's directions. Pour plaster into box, filling to edge of foil. When the plaster has started to thicken, insert trunk, making sure it stands straight. Support the trunk as shown, until plaster has set.

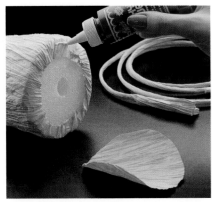

4 Glue the paper twist around cone, piecing as necessary to cover the Styrofoam. Cut a circle of paper twist to the diameter of cone base; glue to bottom of cone. Spray the cone with aerosol acrylic paint, if desired.

5 Glue jeweled garland and cording alternately to cone in continuous rows, starting at lower edge; glue one row at a time. Continue until the cone is completely covered; add another garland, if necessary.

6 Apply hot glue into the hole in the Styrofoam cone and to the top of the trunk. Place cone on trunk.

7 Pin the circles right sides together; stitch ¼" (6 mm) from edge. Turn fabric circle right side out through the slit in lining; press.

8 Wrap the fabric circle around base of tree; secure around dowel with rubber band. Knot ends of cording; wrap the cording around the fabric circle, concealing the rubber band. Embellish tree with star or miniature decorations, if desired, securing them with hot glue.

SHINGLED TREES

Make a grouping of woodland trees in various sizes to accent a holiday table or to display on a mantel. The trees are made using Styrofoam® cones and miniature wooden shingles. For additional color and texture, the trees can be trimmed with wooden cutouts, such as stars, birds, or snowflakes. Or embellish them with miniature beaded garlands.

MATERIALS

- Styrofoam cone, with height of 6" (15 cm), 9" (23 cm), or 12" (30.5 cm), depending on desired tree size.
- Miniature wooden shingles.
- Green paper twist.

- Green acrylic paint; soft-bristled paintbrush.
- Hot glue gun and glue sticks.
- Embellishments, such as miniature wooden cutouts or beaded garland.

HOW TO MAKE A SHINGLED TREE

1 Glue paper twist around cone, piecing as necessary to cover Styrofoam. Cut a circle of paper twist to diameter of cone base; glue to bottom of cone.

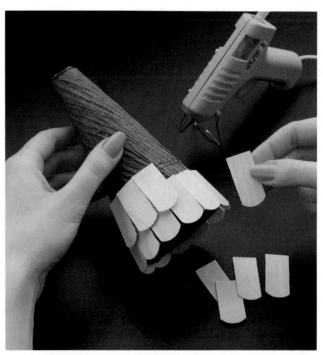

2 Apply hot glue to lower edge of paper-wrapped cone, gluing about 4" (10 cm) at a time. Secure a row of shingles around cone, with the lower edge of the shingles extending about 3/8" (1 cm) below cone. Glue a second row, overlapping shingles about one-half the length of the shingle and staggering placement as shown.

(Continued)

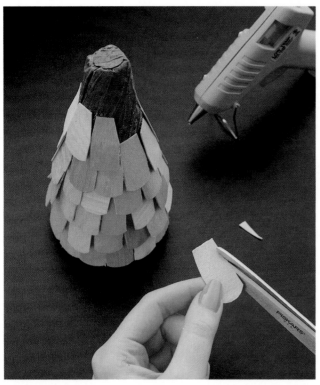

3 Continue applying rows of shingles, overlapping upper edges of shingles at sides as necessary. At upper portion of tree, clip corners of shingles as necessary.

4 Trim four shingles to a point at upper edge as shown, using utility scissors. Glue trimmed shingles to top of cone to complete tree.

5 Dilute green acrylic paint with water. Apply thinned paint liberally to tree, taking care to apply paint to underside of shingles where underside is visible.

6 Embellish tree as desired with wooden cutouts or beaded garland.

TIERED
WOOD
TREES

An easy woodworking project, the tiered wood Christmas tree is made by stacking graduated lengths of screen molding on a wooden dowel. The branches of the tree are movable, allowing for ease in storage. Supplies for the tiered tree can be purchased at craft or lumber supply stores. Finished trees can be decorated with miniature ornaments or garlands, if desired. Unadorned trees are suitable for seasonal decorating all winter.

MATERIALS

- Three 8' (244 cm) lengths screen molding.
- Jigsaw, drill and ¼" drill bit.
- Fine-grit sandpaper; file
- ¼" (6 mm) wooden dowel.
- Wooden block, 1½" (3.8 cm) square.
- Wooden ball knob, 1¼" (3.2 cm) in diameter.
- Wooden base in desired shape, 5" to 7" (12.5 to 18 cm) wide.
- Wood stain; soft cloth.
- Wood glue.
- Miniature ornaments or garlands, optional.

CUTTING DIRECTIONS

Cut each 8' (244 cm) length of screen molding into eight 12" (30.5 cm) pieces. Reserve three 12" 30.5 cm) pieces for the lower branches. Cut off and discard 1" (2.5 cm) from three pieces, to make three 11" (28 cm) branches.

Cut the remaining pieces into four branches each, of the following lengths: 10" (25.5 cm), 9" (23 cm), 8" (20.5 cm), 7" (18 cm), 6" (15 cm), 5" (12.5 cm), 4" (10 cm), 3" (7.5 cm), and 2" (5 cm).

HOW TO MAKE A TIERED WOOD TREE

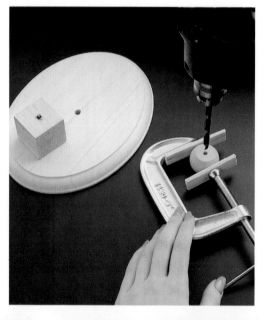

1 Drill hole through center of each branch, using ¼" drill bit. Sand all surfaces of the branches, using fine-grit sandpaper; use file to smooth the rough edges around hole.

2 Drill hole through the center of wooden block, using ¼" drill bit; repeat for wooden base. Enlarge hole in wooden ball knob, using ¼" drill bit and drilling about ⅜" (1 cm) into ball knob; hold the knob securely in the clamp, using scraps of wood to protect sides. Sand the wooden block, base, and ball knob, using sandpaper.

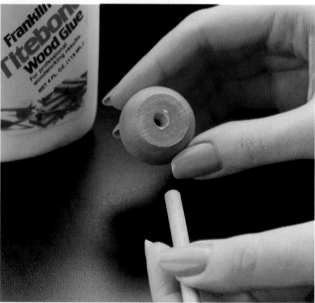

3 Stain all pieces of tree with wood stain, applying stain with soft cloth, following manufacturer's directions. Allow to dry.

4 Apply wood glue to hole in ball knob; insert the end of ¼" (6 mm) wooden dowel into hole.

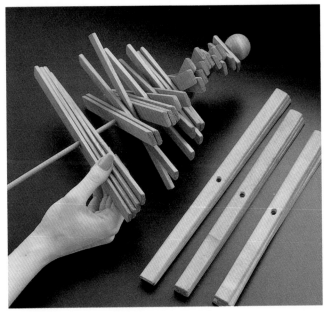

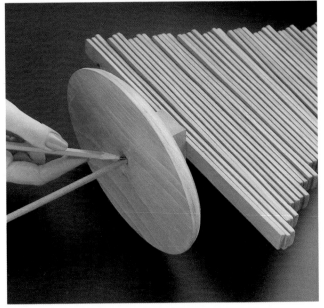

5 Slide tree branches onto dowel, beginning with 2" (5 cm) branches and continuing in order, according to size; keep rounded side of branches facing toward top of tree.

6 Slide wooden block onto dowel; slide wooden base onto dowel. Check to see that all pieces stack snugly together; mark dowel where it exits bottom of base.

7 Remove base; cut dowel at mark.

9 Spread branches of tree in pleasing arrangement. Decorate with miniature ornaments or garlands, if desired.

8 Apply wood glue to the bottom of wooden block and around end of wooden dowel. Insert dowel into hole in base; position block as desired. Allow glue to dry.

BIAS-TRIMMED STOCKINGS

Large stockings, waiting to be filled with candy and trinkets, set the mood for the holiday season. A bias-trimmed stocking can be made in a variety of styles, depending on the choice of fabric and types of embellishments used. For a simple stocking, choose fabric that is distinctive and add embellishments such as purchased appliqués, ribbons, and buttons.

Make the binding from matching or contrasting fabric; a striped or plaid fabric can be used to create interesting effects. The stocking is lined and has a layer of fleece for added body.

MATERIALS

- ¾ yd. (0.7 m) outer fabric.
- ¾ yd. (0.7 m) lining fabric.
- ½ yd. (0.5 m) fabric, for bias binding.
- Polyester fleece.
- Embellishments, such as purchased appliqués, ribbon, or buttons.

CUTTING DIRECTIONS

Make the stocking pattern (below). With the right sides of the fabric together, cut two stocking pieces from the outer fabric and two from the lining. Also cut two stocking pieces from polyester fleece. Cut bias fabric strips, 2½" (6.5 cm) wide, for the binding, cutting two 10" (25.5 cm) strips for the upper edges of the stocking and one 60" (152.5 cm) strip for the sides. Piece the strips as necessary, as on page 52, step 7.

HOW TO MAKE A STOCKING PATTERN

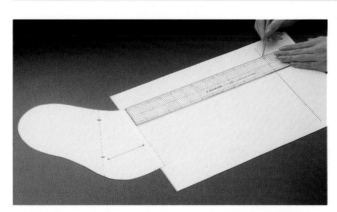

1 Transfer partial pattern pieces A and B (page 153) to paper. Tape pieces together, matching notches. Tape a large piece of paper to upper edge of partial stocking. Draw a line parallel to and 13" (33 cm) above dotted line, to mark upper edge of stocking. Align quilter's ruler to dotted line at side; mark point on line for upper edge. Repeat for the other side.

2 Measure out ⅞" (2.2 cm) from the marked points; mark. Connect the outer points at the upper edge to sides at ends of dotted line, to make full-size stocking pattern.

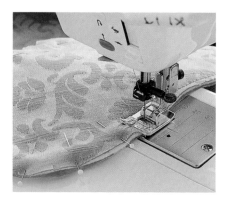

1 Layer the stocking front, fleece, and lining, right sides out. Baste layers together a scant ¼" (6 mm) from raw edges. Repeat for stocking back.

2 Position flat embellishments on the stocking as desired; pin or glue-baste in place. Stitch close to edges of trims.

3 Press the binding strips in half lengthwise, wrong sides together. Pin one 10" (25.5 cm) binding strip to upper edge of stocking front, right sides together, matching raw edges; stitch scant ⅜" (1 cm) seam.

4 Wrap binding around upper edge, covering stitching line on back of stocking; pin. Stitch in the ditch on the right side of stocking, catching binding on stocking back. Trim ends of binding even with stocking. Apply binding to upper edge of stocking back.

5 Align stocking front and back, with lining sides together; pin. Pin the binding to the stocking front, matching raw edges, with right sides together and ends extending ¾" (2 cm) on toe side of the stocking and 6" (15 cm) on the heel side; excess binding on the heel side becomes the hanger. Stitch scant ⅜" (1 cm) from raw edges; ease binding at heel and toe.

6 Fold the short end of the binding over upper edge of stocking. Wrap the binding around edge of stocking, covering stitching line on back; pin.

7 Fold up ½" (1.3 cm) on the end of the extended binding. Press up ¼" (6 mm) on raw edges of the extended binding. Fold the binding in half lengthwise, encasing the raw edges; pin. Edgestitch along pinned edges of the binding, for hanger. Stitch in the ditch around remainder of binding as in step 4.

8 Fold the extended binding strip to the back of stocking, forming a loop for hanger. Hand-stitch in place.

9 Hand-stitch ribbons, bows, or other embellishments to stocking front, if desired.

MORE IDEAS FOR BIAS-TRIMMED STOCKINGS

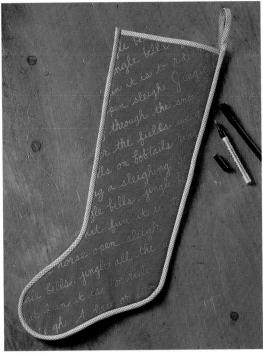

Written verses from "Jingle Bells" cover the front of this stocking. The verses are written using fine-point permanent-ink markers.

Buttons, stitched to the top of the stocking, give the appearance of a cuff.

Tea-dyed fabrics give a homespun look to this stocking. Fused appliqués are applied to the stocking front, using paper-backed fusible web as on pages 50 and 52. Fabric paint is used to personalize the stocking.

WOOLEN STOCKINGS

Turn woolen socks into personalized, one-of-a-kind Christmas stockings. Right at home hanging on a mantel, they also make a fun accent hung from an armoire.

Choose trims that complement the homespun look of the stockings. Add patches of flannel or wool fabric, and trims such as buttons, bells, or fringe. For a cuff, simply turn down the top of the sock. Or hand-stitch a fabric cuff to the top of the stocking. Most items can be stitched in place using a darning needle and narrow ribbon, yarn, or pearl cotton.

Wool socks are available at stores specializing in outdoor clothing. For extra-long stockings, purchase cross-country ski socks.

Woolen stockings can be decorated for a variety of looks. Opposite, a stocking is embellished with sprigs of greenery and cones. Another features a snowman design, stitched in place using blanket stitches. Above, stockings are custom-designed for family pets.

TIPS FOR MAKING WOOLEN STOCKINGS

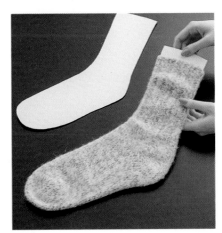

Insert a cardboard liner, cut slightly larger than the sock, into the sock before decorating with hand stitching; the liner will prevent catching stitches in the back of the sock.

Stitch letters, using yarn and backstitches; secure stitches by taking one or two concealed small stitches.

Knot a loop of ribbon through top of sock for a hanger. Stuff finished stocking with tissue paper or with polyester fiberfill.

SANTA'S ELVES

Pose an elf or two on a table or mantel to add a whimsical touch to your holiday decorating. The body of the elf is stuffed with polyester fiberfill and is weighted down with a small bag of sand. Small quantities of sand are available, packaged as paint additives, at many paint stores.

MATERIALS

- Fabric scraps.
- 3" (7.5 cm) square of paper-backed fusible web.
- Assorted two-hole or four-hole buttons.
- Two small shank buttons, for eyes.
- Polyester fiberfill.
- Sand; plastic bag, such as a sandwich bag.
- Jute and ¼" (6 mm) dowel, for hair.
- Hot glue gun and glue sticks.
- Heavy-duty thread, such as carpet thread.
- Pink cosmetic blush.
- Embellishments as desired.

CUTTING DIRECTIONS

Make the full-size patterns for the upper body, lower body, and hat as in steps 1 to 3, opposite. Cut two lower body pieces and two upper body pieces from scraps of fabric for the body. Using the pattern for the upper body, also cut two hat pieces from scraps of fabric for the hat.

Trace the pattern pieces for the boot and ear (page 152) onto paper. Cut four boots and four ears from scraps of fabric.

For the pants legs, cut two 5½" × 6" (14 × 15 cm) rectangles from scraps of fabric that match the lower body. For the sleeves, cut two 4½" × 5½" (11.5 × 14 cm) rectangles from scraps of fabric that match the upper body.

1 Draw a 9½" (24.3 cm) vertical line on center of tracing paper. Draw a perpendicular line at lower end, 3¼" (8.2 cm) long. Mark a point 3½" (9 cm) above lower edge and 2½" (6.5 cm) from vertical line. Mark a second point 6½" (16.3 cm) above lower edge and 1¾" (4.5 cm) from vertical line.

2 Connect points to perpendicular lines, curving the line slightly. Fold on vertical line; cut on the marked lines. Unfold paper.

3 Draw line 3½" (9 cm) above lower edge, perpendicular to vertical line. Cut off lower portion on marked line; this section is pattern for lower body of elf. Remaining section is pattern for upper body and also for hat. Transfer the patterns to paper, adding ¼" (6 mm) seam allowances.

4 Cut body pieces from fabric (opposite). Apply paper-backed fusible web to scrap of fabric for face, following manufacturer's directions. Cut an oval for face, about 2" (5 cm) long and 2¼" (6 cm) wide, from paper-backed fabric.

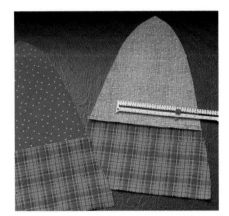  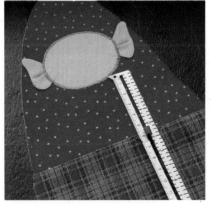

5 Align upper and lower front body sections, right sides together; stitch ¼" (6 mm) seam. Repeat for the back body sections, leaving a 3" (7.5 cm) opening in center of seam.

6 Stitch ⅛" (3 mm) seam around the ears, using short stitch length; leave straight edges open. Turn ears right side out, and press. Using cotton swab, rub pink blush in center of ears.

7 Remove paper backing from face. Make ⅛" (3 mm) tuck along the straight edge of each ear; baste to wrong side of face. Center face on upper body, with the face about 2¼" (6 cm) above the body seam. Fuse in place. Stitch around the face, using a narrow zigzag stitch.

(Continued)

8 Fold rectangle for sleeve in half, right sides together, matching short edges; stitch ¼" (6 mm) seam. Press seam open; turn tube right side out. Center the seam down front of tube. Make four ⅛" (3 mm) tucks, spaced evenly along upper edge of tube, so width is about 1½" (3.8 cm).

9 Pin tucked end of sleeve, seam side down, to right side of front upper body; match raw edges, and position sleeve about 1" (2.5 cm) above body seam. Baste. Repeat for other sleeve.

10 Fold rectangle for pants leg, right sides together, matching short edges; stitch ¼" (6 mm) seam. Press seam open; turn tube right side out. Center seam down back of tube. Repeat for other pants leg. Pin upper edge of pants legs to lower edge of front body section, centering them and matching raw edges; baste.

11 Pin front and back body sections right sides together. Stitch ¼" (6 mm) seam around body, taking care not to catch sleeves, pants legs, and ears in stitching.

12 Push in lower corners of elf, from right side, to shape the box corners. Slipstitch, or turn inside out and machine-stitch, across corners; turn right side out.

13 Roll up sleeves and pants legs. Thread needle with heavy-duty thread; secure thread to body, centered inside one pants leg. Thread a 2¾" (7 cm) strand of buttons, then thread back through the opposite holes of buttons; adjust the strand so top button of strand dangles about 3" (7.5 cm) below body. Secure thread. Repeat for other leg.

14 Stuff pants legs lightly with polyester fiberfill. On each pants leg, fold lower ¼" (6 mm) to the inside. Using hand running stitches, stitch close to the fold and tightly gather pants legs above buttons; secure thread.

15 Stitch ⅛" (3 mm) seam around the boot, using short stitch length; leave upper edge open. Clip inner curve. Turn right side out; stuff with polyester fiberfill. On each boot, fold upper ¼" (6 mm) to inside; slipstitch closed. Stitch the center of each boot to lower button of each button strand for legs.

16 Secure heavy-duty thread to body, centered inside one sleeve. Thread a 3" (7.5 cm) strand of buttons; secure thread inside other sleeve, allowing button strand to dangle from body about 2" (5 cm) at each side. Stuff sleeves and gather above buttons as in step 14.

17 Place about ⅔ cup (150 mL) sand in plastic bag. Tape bag closed, allowing space inside for sand to shift easily; this makes it easier for elf to sit. Insert the bag into the lower portion of body. Stuff remainder of body with polyester fiberfill; slipstitch opening closed.

18 Sew on buttons for the eyes; insert needle from back of body, and pull thread taut for a slight indentation. Rub pink blush on the face, for cheeks. Make jute hair, if desired, as on page 14, step 15; remove jute from dowel. Cut lengths of jute, and glue around face for the hair and beard.

19 Pin the hat pieces right sides together; stitch ¼" (6 mm) seam around curved sides. Turn right side out. Sew on buttons as desired at top of hat. Fold lower ¼" (6 mm) of hat to inside. Using hand running stitches, stitch close to fold; gather hat to fit head. Glue the hat to the elf. Secure any additional embellishments.

Create a winter scene with a wooden cutout village. This village is easily made using basic carpentry skills. Distressed edges and antiquing emphasize the handcrafted quality of the pieces.

The village pieces are made from scraps of pine lumber. Pine is easily cut with a jigsaw, and any imperfections in cutting can be sanded smooth. It is not necessary for the pieces to be cut symmetrically. Subtle variations add to the style. When cutting with a jigsaw, clamp the wood in place, protecting it, if necessary, by placing scrap blocks of wood or small felt pads between the workpiece and the clamp. Hold the saw tightly against the workpiece to reduce vibration, and move the saw smoothly while cutting. Cut curves with a fine-toothed scroll-cut blade, and use a slower speed to avoid bending the blade.

To give the cutouts an old-fashioned country look, paint them with acrylic paints in muted colors. Use off-white paint for the snowman and spattered snow.

MATERIALS

- Scraps of pine lumber: 2 × 8 pine lumber for house and large tree; 1 × 6 for small tree; 1 × 4 for snowman.
- Jigsaw; drill and ³⁄₃₂" drill bit.
- Sanding block; medium-grit and fine-grit sandpaper.
- Acrylic paints; artist's brushes.
- 1" or 1½" (2.5 or 3.8 cm) synthetic-bristle paintbrush, for spattering.
- Transfer paper; masking tape, mat knife; wood glue or thick craft glue; hot glue gun and glue sticks.
- Stain in medium color, such as medium walnut.
- Embellishments for house, such as a miniature wreath or garland.
- Round toothpick and scrap of fabric, for snowman.
- Balsa wood molding strip in ⅛" (3 mm) thickness and desired width, for flower boxes.

HOW TO MAKE A WOODEN CUTOUT HOUSE

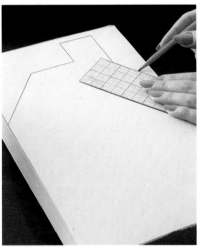

1 Cut a sheet of paper to width of 2 × 8 board and about 12" (30.5 cm) high. Draw roofline and chimney, using guide on page 157. Transfer guideline to wood, using transfer paper.

2 Cut along the marked lines, using jigsaw. Sand the wood smooth, using medium-grit sandpaper. Fold the sandpaper in thirds to sand the corners, curves, and edges.

3 Mark doors and windows on front of house as desired, using masking tape. Mark mullions, using ¼" (6 mm) strips of masking tape.

4 Mark the roofline with masking tape. Cut window boxes to size from balsa wood, using mat knife.

5 Paint the doors, windows, roof, and window boxes as desired. Allow to dry; remove tape. Paint chimney; add random strokes to represent bricks.

(Continued)

97

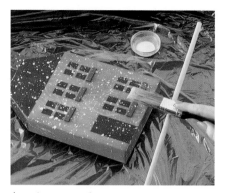

6 Sand edges of house and window boxes lightly, using a fine-grit sandpaper, to remove some paint and give an aged look. Apply stain to all pieces, using soft cloth; allow to dry. Secure window boxes with wood glue or thick craft glue.

7 Thin paint for snow, mixing two parts paint with one part water. Protect work surface with drop cloths or newspapers. Dip tip of brush into paint. Hold stick and paintbrush over project; strike brush handle against stick to spatter paint.

8 Place wreath over door; secure with hot glue. Attach additional embellishments as desired.

HOW TO MAKE A WOODEN CUTOUT SNOWMAN

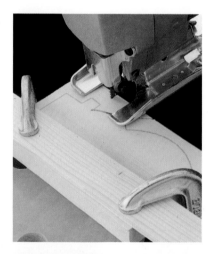

1 Trace pattern (page 157) onto paper. Transfer pattern to wood, using transfer paper.

2 Cut along the marked lines, using a jigsaw. Starting at edge of board, cut along the upper half of top curve. Then, starting at edge of board, cut along lower edge of hat; this will remove wedge of wood. Continue cutting out remainder of snowman.

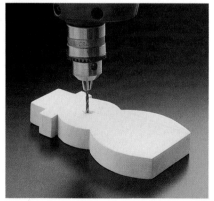

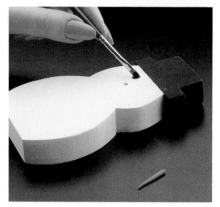

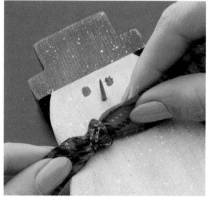

3 Sand the snowman as on page 97, step 2. Using a 3/32" drill bit, drill hole about 3/8" (1 cm) deep, for nose.

4 Paint the snowman, using artist's brush. Break off 7/8" (2.2 cm) length of toothpick; paint orange. Transfer markings for eyes, if desired, using transfer paper. Paint eyes.

5 Follow step 6 above; insert the toothpick nose into the hole, gluing in place. Continue as in step 7, above. Cut 3/4" × 12" (2 × 30.5 cm) fabric strip; tie around neck, for scarf.

HOW TO MAKE A WOODEN CUTOUT TREE

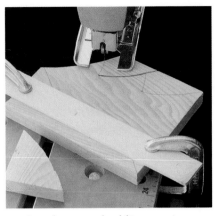

1 Trace desired tree pattern (page 156) onto paper; fold paper on the dotted line. Cut on the marked line to make full-size pattern. Transfer the pattern to wood, using transfer paper.

2 Cut along marked lines, using a jigsaw; cut curves from the edge of board to inside corners.

3 Sand the tree as on page 97, step 2. Paint the tree, using artist's brush, allowing the grain of wood to show through in some areas. Complete the tree as in steps 6 and 7, opposite.

MORE IDEAS FOR WOODEN CUTOUTS

Gingerbread house *is decorated with purchased wooden cutouts and painted candy canes.*

Personalized house *is painted to resemble the owner's home. Snow paste adds texture to the roof.*

Wooden blocks, *cut from a 2 × 4 board, are painted with simple lettering and Christmas motifs for a holiday display.*

Gift Giving
& Cards

PINECONE KINDLERS
&0

Place kindler under
firewood and light.

HAPPY HOLIDAYS

PINECONE KINDLERS

For an inexpensive gift that is both useful and decorative, fill a basket with pinecone kindlers. Pinecones are dipped in melted paraffin wax and cooled in metal or glass muffin cups atop shallow paraffin wax bases. Candlewicks running through the bases keep the pinecones burning for up to twenty minutes, while kindling logs for the fire. Paraffin for the pinecone kindlers can be colored red and scented with cinnamon, or colored green and scented with pine, if desired. To light a fire, center a pinecone kindler under stacked firewood and light the wick.

MATERIALS

- Double boiler.
- Paraffin wax, approximately 1 lb. (450 g) per six pinecones.
- Candle color squares and candle scent squares, one square each per pound (450 g) of paraffin wax.
- Candy thermometer.
- Muffin tin.
- Nonstick vegetable oil spray.
- Wax-coated candlewicks, 6" (15 cm) long.
- Pinecones, 2" (5 cm) in diameter or size to fit muffin cups.
- Tongs.

HOW TO MAKE PINECONE KINDLERS

1 Insert candy thermometer into double boiler. Melt one pound (450 g) paraffin wax in top of double boiler over boiling water. Add one square of the candle color and one square of the candle scent as desired. Mix gently, using wooden spoon.

2 Spray the muffin cups lightly with nonstick vegetable oil spray. Place one end of wax-coated candlewick in each muffin cup; allow opposite end to hang over side of muffin cup.

3 Cool melted paraffin to about 160°F (70°C). Dip pinecone in paraffin, turning to coat thoroughly. Raise pinecone above wax for a few seconds, allowing parafin to harden; repeat two or three times. Remove with tongs, and place coated pinecone upright in muffin cup over candlewick.

4 Remove top pan of double boiler containing remaining melted paraffin. Dry outside of pan with towel to prevent water from dripping into muffin cups. Slowly pour ½" (1.3 cm) melted paraffin into each muffin cup at base of pinecone.

5 Allow the kindlers to cool completely. Remove from muffin cups. Arrange in decorative gift basket; prepare note card with instructions for use.

WOODEN BASKETS

Handcrafted wooden baskets are ideal for gift giving and can be used as decorative accents throughout the holiday season. Make the baskets using either a snowman or a Christmas tree design. An aged look, achieved by sanding the edges and applying stain, gives the baskets a rustic charm. They are inexpensive to make and require only basic woodworking skills and tools.

When cutting with a jigsaw, it is helpful to clamp the wood in place, protecting it with wood scraps or felt pads, if necessary. This also allows you to hold the saw firmly with both hands, to reduce vibration, and move the saw smoothly while cutting. Cut inside corners by sawing into the corner from both directions; cut curves slowly to avoid bending the blade.

MATERIALS

- 12 ft. (3.7 m) of ¼" × ¾" (6 mm × 2 cm) pine screen molding.
- 1 × 8 pine board.
- Wooden dowel, ½" (1.3 cm) diameter, 11¼" (28.7 cm) long.
- Jigsaw.
- Drill; ¹⁄₁₆" and ½" drill bits.
- Sanding block; medium-grit and fine-grit sandpaper.
- Acrylic paints; artist's brushes.
- Stain in medium color, such as medium walnut.
- 17 × ¾" (2 cm) brads.
- Wood glue; tracing paper; graphite paper.
- Scrap of wool fabric, for snowman scarf, optional.

HOW TO MAKE A WOODEN BASKET

1 Fold sheet of tracing paper in half lengthwise. Trace the partial pattern (page 155) for tree or snowman onto tracing paper, placing fold of tracing paper on dotted line of pattern. Cut out pattern. Open the full-size pattern. Transfer the pattern to 1 × 8 pine board twice; align the arrow on pattern with grain of wood. Transfer mark for handle.

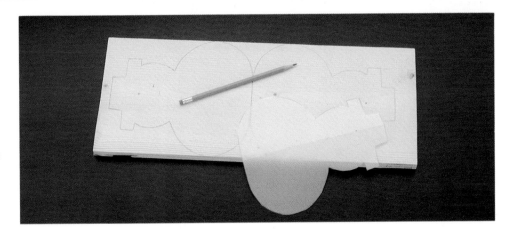

(Continued)

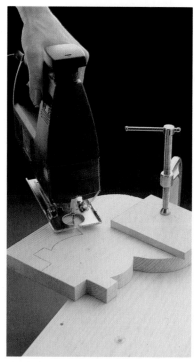

2 Cut along marked lines, using jigsaw.

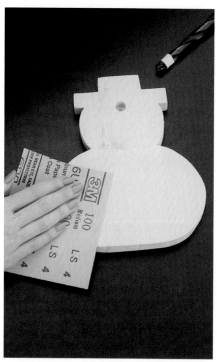

3 Drill hole at mark for handle to ⅜" (1 cm) depth, using ½" drill bit; use masking tape on drill bit as guide for the depth. Sand basket ends smooth, using medium-grit sandpaper.

4 Mark and cut twelve slats from screen molding, in 12" (30.5 cm) lengths. Sand ends. Predrill nail holes ⅜" (1 cm) from each end of each slat, using ¹⁄₁₆" drill bit.

5 Paint outer surface of basket ends as desired, using acrylic paints and foam applicator. Allow to dry.

6 Sand edges of the basket ends lightly, using fine-grit sandpaper, to remove some paint and give an aged appearance.

7 Apply stain to all pieces, using soft cloth; allow to dry.

8 Mark placement for slats on the basket ends, using pattern as guide. Secure slats to one basket end, using 17 × ¾" (2 cm) brads; align the end of slat to outer edge of basket end, with the rounded edges of the slat facing outward.

9 Apply small amount of wood glue in the holes for handle. Insert dowel ends into holes.

10 Secure slats to remaining basket end. For snowman basket, cut two 1½" × 22" (3.8 × 56 cm) fabric strips; clip ends to make fringe, and tie around necks, for scarves.

QUICK & EASY GIFT IDEAS

For handcrafted gifts that are simple to make, try a delicate Christmas potpourri, an herbal cooking oil, or a decorative painted candle. For potpourri, use the recipe opposite for a mixture with a dominant pine scent. Or vary the floral elements and use an essential oil of your choice. When varying the recipe, always remember to use a fixative, since this is the ingredient that helps the potpourri retain its scent.

Herbal cooking oil can easily be made in a few minutes; however, it must sit for about three weeks before it can be used. To help distribute the flavor, shake the bottle every few days. The flavor becomes stronger, the longer it sits.

Easy-to-make painted candles can become personalized gifts. Decorate them with Christmas motifs, favorite verses from Christmas carols, or personal names.

Painted candles (*opposite*) *are decorated in the holiday spirit. Select pillar candles with smooth surfaces, and embellish as desired with craft acrylic paints. Add dimensional detail with acrylic paints in fine-tip tubes. Or add sparkle with glitter glue.*

Herbal cooking oils (*right*) *are great gift ideas for the cooking enthusiast. Wash and dry fresh herbs, such as rosemary, tarragon, thyme, basil, or dill; then place about three sprigs of the selected herb in a decorative bottle. Fill the bottle with a cooking oil, such as olive oil or corn oil; then cap the bottle with a cork and allow to sit at room temperature for about three weeks. Homemade cooking oils should be used immediately when ready. Keep oil stored in the refrigerator.*

CHRISTMAS POTPOURRI

1 qt. (1 L) mixture of small pinecones, star anise, juniper berries, red rose petals, green eucalyptus, and cedar needles.

10 to 15 red rose heads or buds.

10 to 12 cinnamon sticks, 3" (7.5 cm) long.

½ teaspoon (2 mL) whole cloves.

Four drops pine essential oil.

Two drops cinnamon essential oil.

Fixative, such as 1 oz. (25 g) orris root powder or ¼ cup (50 mL) cut orris root, chopped calamus, or cellulose-fiber fixative.

Place fixative in bowl and add drops of essential oils. Mix thoroughly, to ensure that scent of oil is fixed. Mix remaining ingredients in large bowl. Add fixative and essential oil mixture to large bowl; mix thoroughly. Place potpourri in airtight container; leave in dark place for at least six weeks. Shake container daily for first week. Package potpourri in a decorative canister to give as a gift, or keep it yourself and display in a decorative open container.

Christmas potpourri (*below*) *makes a decorative room accent and provides a pleasant aroma.*

FABRIC GIFT WRAPS

Wrap packages creatively with fabric gift wraps. Choose from three styles, including circular gift wraps, rolled gift wraps, or gift bags. Make the gift wraps from lightweight to mediumweight fabrics, such as satin, taffeta, lamé, or seasonal broadcloth prints. Line the gift wraps with contrasting fabrics; the wraps can then be reversed and used with different trimmings for a new look for the following year. Embellish the gift wraps with coordinating trims, such as wired ribbon or cording. Purchased end caps may be applied to the ends of the cording, if desired.

The circular gift wrap is ideal for baked goods and soft garment accessories, such as slippers, mittens, or socks. The rolled gift wrap works well for soft gift items, such as articles of clothing, that can be folded into rectangles. Custom-sized gift bags can be used for bottles and other items that are difficult to wrap.

CUTTING DIRECTIONS

For the circular gift wrap, cut one circle each from outer fabric and lining as on page 112, steps 1 and 2.

For the rolled gift wrap, cut one rectangle each from outer fabric and lining, 4" (10 cm) larger than gift on all sides.

For the gift bag, cut two rectangles each from outer fabric and lining, using the method on page 113, step 1, to determine the size of the rectangles.

MATERIALS

- Fabrics, for gift wrap and contrasting lining.
- Rubber band.
- Ribbon or cording.
- End caps, for cording, optional.

HOW TO SEW A CIRCULAR GIFT WRAP

1 Position the gift as it will be placed in center of gift wrap. Determine diameter of the circle by measuring around the gift as shown and adding 4" to 10" (10 to 25 cm) for heading and seam allowances.

2 Fold outer fabric in half lengthwise, then crosswise. Using a straightedge and pencil, mark an arc on fabric, measuring one-half desired diameter of circle from folded center of fabric. Cut on marked line through all layers; mark raw edge at foldlines. Cut lining to same size; mark.

3 Pin the outer fabric to lining, right sides together, matching marks; stitch ¼" (6 mm) from raw edges, leaving 4" (10 cm) opening for turning.

4 Turn right side out; press. Slipstitch opening closed. Center the gift on the fabric. Draw fabric around gift, securing it with rubber band. Adjust folds; tie ribbon or cording around top, concealing rubber band.

HOW TO SEW A ROLLED GIFT WRAP

1 Pin outer fabric to lining, right sides together, stitch ¼" (6 mm) from raw edges, leaving 4" (10 cm) opening for turning.

2 Turn the rectangle right side out; press. Slipstitch the opening closed. Center gift on fabric, allowing space around all sides. Roll up rectangle.

3 Draw up fabric at ends, securing it with rubber bands. Adjust folds; tie cording or ribbon around ends, concealing rubber band.

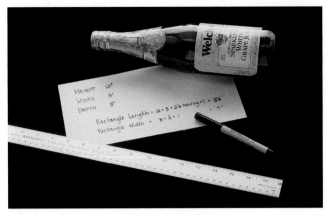

1 Measure height, width, and depth of gift as it will be inserted in the gift bag; record these measurements. Determine the size of rectangles for gift bag, with length equal to height and depth of gift plus desired heading plus 1" (2.5 cm); width of rectangle is equal to width and depth of gift plus 1" (2.5 cm).

2 Cut rectangles from the outer fabric and lining as determined in step 1. Pin the rectangles right sides together; stitch ¼" (6 mm) from raw edges, leaving top of gift bag open. Repeat for lining, leaving 3" (7.5 cm) opening on one side near top.

3 Fold gift bag at bottom so side seam is aligned to the bottom seam; pin. Measure from the corner across seams a distance equal to one-half the depth of the gift; mark a point on seamline. Draw a line through point, perpendicular to seamline.

4 Stitch along marked line; trim close to the stitching. Repeat steps 3 and 4 for opposite corner, and repeat for corners of lining.

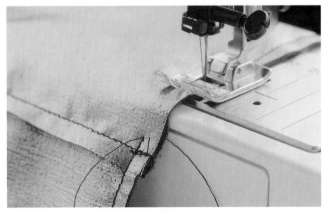

5 Place outer bag inside the lining, right sides together. Pin upper edges, raw edges even; stitch ¼" (6 mm) from edge. Turn right side out through opening in lining. Hand-stitch opening closed.

6 Insert lining; lightly press upper edge. Insert the gift into bag; draw fabric up around gift, securing it with a rubber band. Tie ribbon or cording around top, concealing rubber band.

STAMPED GIFT WRAPS

Make your own rubber stamps, and turn plain paper and bags into one-of-a-kind gift wraps. The stamps can also be used to embellish tissue paper and ribbons.

Stamps are made by cutting designs into artist's erasers or printing blocks, using a sharp mat knife. For easier cutting, select designs with simple details.

Stamp pads are available at art supply stores and print shops. Some metallic inks may leave oil marks on fabric ribbons. For best results, apply spray starch heavily to fabric ribbons and press them with an iron before stamping the designs.

MATERIALS

- Soft artist's eraser or printing block.
- Tracing paper.
- Transfer paper.
- Mat knife.
- Stamp pad.
- Plain wrapping paper, tissue paper, paper bags, and ribbons as desired.

HOW TO MAKE STAMPED GIFT WRAPS

1 Trace design onto paper. Transfer to smooth side of artist's eraser or printing block, using the transfer paper. Cut about ⅛" (3 mm) deep into eraser along design lines, using mat knife.

2 Remove large background area around design by cutting horizontally through the edge of eraser and up to the cuts made for the design outline.

3 Cut and remove narrow spaces within design, by cutting at an angle along each edge; remove the small background areas.

4 Press the stamp firmly onto the stamp pad; lift and repeat as necessary until the design on the stamp is evenly coated. Press stamp straight down onto paper or ribbon, using even pressure.

RIBBON GIFT-BOWS

Packages wrapped with lavish bows make beautiful displays beneath the tree and entice the gift recipient. Ribbon gift-bows are simple to make and suitable for many types of ribbon, including wired ribbon, sinamay ribbon, paper twist, and metallic twist.

The bow is assembled using a stapler. For best results, use a hand stapler. This style stapler, available at office supply stores, allows you to secure the ribbon snugly around the box. Each bow requires about 2½ yd. (2.3 m) of ribbon, plus the amount needed to wrap around the box.

When selecting papers, think beyond the typical wrapping papers. Papers such as plain white and brown paper, printed newspaper, parchment paper, and decorative tissue papers make packages unique. Materials such as corrugated cardboard, fabric, and cellophane can also be used. For additional embellishment, personalize the package with an ornament or sprig of greenery.

MATERIALS

• Ribbon.   • Hand stapler.

HOW TO MAKE A RIBBON GIFT-BOW

1 Wrap ribbon around box in one direction; secure with staple. Trim excess ribbon.

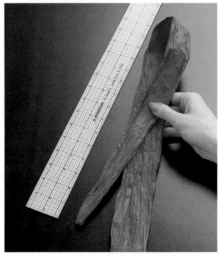

2 Form ribbon into a 5½" to 6" (14 to 15 cm) loop as shown, allowing about an 8" (20.5 cm) tail and taking care that the right side of the ribbon is facing out.

3 Fold a loop toward the opposite side, bringing ribbon over tail to keep right side of ribbon facing out.

4 Continue wrapping ribbon to form two loops on each side with a second tail extending. Position bow over ribbon on package; secure with one or two staples at center.

5 Tie about a 24" (61 cm) length of ribbon around center of bow, knotting it on back of bow. Trim tails as desired.

QUICK & EASY GIFT WRAPPING

For unique gift wrapping, personalize a variety of simple bags or containers. Choose from buckets, pine bandboxes, lunch bags, or shopping bags. These types of packaging can often be kept for future use. Embellish the packaging with painted designs, stickers, floral materials, or even a keepsake ornament.

Personalized gift wrap *is easy to create. Above, the tin bucket is painted to make a keepsake container for a child's gift. Lunch bags, embellished with stickers, become personalized packages, and holiday shoelaces replace a traditional ribbon on a Christmas gift. Opposite, a bandbox is embellished with a cluster of ribbon roses for a romantic package. Beeswax ornaments, made by pouring melted wax into molds, decorate a plain brown-paper gift bag. Wine-bottle bag, sprayed with silver and gold paint, becomes an instant gift bag. Cardboard tubes, concealing small gifts, are wrapped to represent Christmas "firecrackers."*

MORE IDEAS
FOR GIFT WRAPS

Shown left to right, top row:

Christmas message *is written across brown paper to make a personalized package.*

Organza ribbon and floral cluster *(page 62) are used as accents on a foil-wrapped package.*

Rows of jute and cotton string *are used in place of ribbon on a brown-paper package, for a natural look.*

Purchased or handmade stocking ornament *is used to decorate a holiday package. The Christmas ornament becomes an extra keepsake gift.*

Shown left to right, bottom row:

Aromatic dough ornament and torn-fabric bow *are used to decorate a package, for a country look.*

Canella berries, greenery, and cones *embellish a brown-paper package that is tied with jute.*

Papier-mâché box, *shaped like a star, is embellished with pieces of imitation gold and silver leaf as on page 38. Ribbons with metallic edgings are used as an accent.*

Lace doily and organza bow *are secured to the lid of a small painted bandbox, for a romantic touch.*

EMBOSSED CARDS

Create personalized holiday greetings by making your own embossed cards and gift tags. The embossed, or raised, design is made by placing paper over a stencil cutout and rubbing along the design with a *stylus,* a hard-pointed, pen-shaped tool. To add sparkle to the card, highlight the embossed design with glitter.

Custom stencils can be created inexpensively using transparent Mylar® sheets, available at craft stores. Designs for stencils can be found on Christmas cards or in stencil design books. Enlarge or reduce the designs, if necessary, on a photocopy machine.

Use card-stock or heavyweight stationery to prevent any tearing during embossing. Most print shops have paper, cards, and envelopes in a variety of weights and colors.

If you are cutting your own cards and tags, cut and fold the paper to the finished size before embossing. If a paper cutter is not available, use a metal straightedge, a mat knife, and a cutting mat.

When tracing around the design areas, it is necessary to place the stencil and paper over an illuminated surface, such as a light box or a sunlit window. If the stylus has two ball ends, use the large end of the stylus for tracing around large design areas and the small end for fine, detailed areas. If the stylus squeaks as it is moved across the paper, lubricate the end by rubbing it in the palm of your hand.

MATERIALS

- Card-stock or heavyweight stationery.
- Transparent Mylar sheets.
- Fine-point permanent-ink marking pen.
- Paper cutter; or mat knife, cutting surface, such as a cutting mat, and metal straightedge.
- Stylus or small plastic crochet hook, for tracing design.
- Removable transparent tape.
- Glue pen, extra-fine glitter, and soft artist's eraser, for glittered cards.
- Light box or other illuminated glass surface.
- Cording, for gift tag.

HOW TO MAKE AN EMBOSSED CARD

1 Position Mylar® over design, allowing a 1" (2.5 cm) border; secure with tape. Trace design, using permanent-ink marking pen; simplify the shapes as necessary.

2 Cut out inner details of the design, using mat knife; use straightedge to cut along the straight lines. Cut and remove the smallest areas first, then larger ones. Pull knife toward you as you cut; turn Mylar, rather than knife, to change directions.

3 Redraw outer lines of design as necessary, to touch up any lines that were removed when cutting. Cut excess Mylar from outer edges of the design, using a mat knife and a straightedge; leave at least ¼" (6 mm) border.

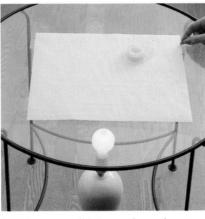

4 Position the stencil as desired on front of card; secure stencil with removable tape.

5 Place a small lamp under a glass-top table if a light box is unavailable. Tape a piece of tracing paper over the glass to act as a light diffuser, if necessary.

6 Place the card, stencil side down, on light table. Using stylus, trace outline of the design, applying firm pressure. Retrace, if necessary, for clear definition. Trace around outer edges of stencil, if desired, to frame the design.

7 Remove stencil. For glittered cards, apply glue to desired design details; sprinkle glitter over the wet glue. Shake off the excess glitter; allow glue to dry. Remove any excess glitter from card, using soft artist's eraser. Personalize card with initials, using a permanent-ink marking pen.

8 Punch hole in upper left corner of card to make gift tag. Cut 8" (20.5 cm) length of cording. Fold cording in half, and insert folded end through tag; bring the cut ends through the loop, and pull to secure.

FIBER-MÂCHÉ CARDS & GIFT TAGS

Create unique cards or gift tags, using a fiber-mâché arts and crafts medium, such as WildFiber™. This material is composed of natural and synthetic fibers, and a non-toxic binder. When combined with water, the fibers adhere to each other, allowing the mixture to be molded or rolled flat to create a substance with the look of handmade paper. WildFiber is available in a wide range of colors at many arts and crafts stores. For dimensional designs, WildFiber can be pressed into plastic molds. Or to create your own flat images, roll the material flat between plastic sheets; allow it to dry. Then cut or tear your own shapes. Use the fiber-mâché shapes as gift tags, or glue them to blank greeting cards to make custom-designed Christmas cards. Blank greeting cards can be found at stationery or office supply stores.

MATERIALS

- Fiber-mâché, such as WildFiber, in desired colors.
- Bowl; craft sticks.
- Paper toweling.
- Plastic-wrapped cardboard, extra plastic.
- Metal cookie cutter, for shapes with torn edges.
- Rolling pin.
- Plastic molds.
- Narrow ribbon or cording, for gift tag; darning needle.
- Craft glue.

HOW TO MAKE MOLDED FIBER-MÂCHÉ CARDS & GIFT TAGS

1 Mix WildFiber with water to create a pastelike consistency. Allow to set 15 minutes, until moisture has been absorbed by fibers.

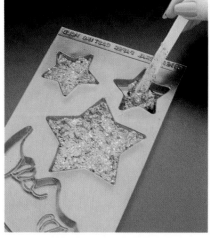

2 Spread and press mixture on the inside surface of the mold with a craft stick, until about 1/8" (3 mm) thick. Place mold in freezer for about 30 minutes to set shape.

3 Carefully remove molded shape from mold; place on several sheets of paper toweling until dry. Secure to blank gift card or piece of decorative paper, using glue. For gift tag, thread cording or narrow ribbon into darning needle; then insert through top of tag, and knot ends.

124

HOW TO MAKE FLAT FIBER-MÂCHÉ CARDS & GIFT TAGS

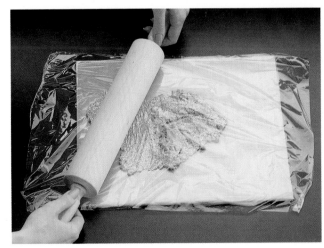

1 Mix WildFiber as in step 1, opposite. Place WildFiber mixture between a piece of plastic-wrapped cardboard and a second piece of plastic; then roll it out to desired thickness with rolling pin. Place in freezer for about 30 minutes. Remove from freezer; let set for 5 minutes.

2 Press imprint of desired shape into fiber-mâché. Allow to dry. Tear or cut along imprint line. Secure to blank gift card or piece of decorative paper, using glue. For gift tag, thread cording or narrow ribbon into darning needle; then insert through top of tag, and knot ends.

MORE IDEAS
FOR CARDS

Gingerbread man is cut from brown paper, using a cookie cutter as a pattern. The card is embellished with buttons, raffia, and fabric paints in fine-tip tubes.

Metal stars (page 33), secured with brass wire to a piece of card-stock paper, become a unique greeting card.

Aromatic dough ornament *(page 42) is glued to a piece of corrugated cardboard, to make a gift tag.*

Fabric motifs *are fused to a blank gift card, using paper-backed fusible web and a dry iron.*

Shipping tag *is used to make the gift tag above. A design is embossed onto the tag as on page 122.*

Victorian cutout *(left) is secured to a piece of metallic tagboard, using spray adhesive. Cut ¼" (6 mm) away from motif, and secure to card-stock paper.*

The Holiday Table

Bias swags *are accented with bows and evergreen boughs to repeat the theme of the table setting.*

Gift-wrapped boxes *(left) are used as risers to create a tiered table setting. A wrapped box with the lid set aside holds rolled napkins tied with ribbons.*

CHRISTMAS BUFFET

The holiday season is a popular time for entertaining. Whether you are planning an open house for your friends or a Christmas Eve buffet for the family, the elegance and richness of burgundy and gold make the buffet table more festive. A combination of Christmas lights and candlelight adds a warm glow, accentuating the rich colors.

Buffet table *is decorated with swagged table linens, wrapped boxes, and evergreen boughs, all accented with burgundy and gold ribbons for a coordinated setting. Christmas lights and votive candles are strewn throughout, to add a warm glow. Brass candlesticks are decorated with branches of mixed evergreens, inserted into floral foam cages.*

Wassail bowl, *surrounded by a cedar wreath, is placed on a separate side table, to avoid congestion at the main buffet table. The wreath is trimmed with Christmas lights to accentuate the golden glow of the wassail.*

Country arrangement *is created by filling small brown bags with popcorn, nuts, and dried fruits. The bags are tied with torn strips of fabric and placed in a rustic basket.*

Elegant decorating accent *is created from a dried grapevine wreath, an artificial vine of grape leaves, dried artichokes, and gilded cones. Refer to pages 60 to 63 for information on embellishing wreaths.*

Natural setting *is created with a pine garland used as the base of the arrangement. Pillar candles placed in glasses and smaller votive candles are embellished with cinnamon sticks and raffia. Spice ornaments and dried flowers are scattered throughout, for additional interest.*

CANDY WREATHS

A candy wreath is a festive holiday decoration full of little gifts. In one version, brightly wrapped Christmas candies nestle among coils of curled ribbon. For a fringed fabric wreath, candies are tied with raffia between knotted strips of cotton fabric. Small scissors hanging from the wreath invite each guest to snip out a piece of candy.

MATERIALS

- Metal ring, 8" (20.5 cm) in diameter.
- 50 to 70 yd. (46 to 64.4 m) curling ribbon in choice of colors, for ribbon wreath.
- ¼ yd. (0.25 m) each of three cotton print fabrics, for fringed fabric wreath.
- Raffia, for fringed fabric wreath.
- Wrapped Christmas candies.
- Small scissors.

HOW TO MAKE A CANDY & RIBBON WREATH

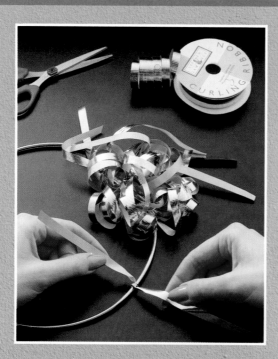

1 Cut a 12" (30.5 cm) length of curling ribbon. Wrap ribbon around metal ring; knot, leaving tails of equal length. Repeat, alternating ribbon colors as desired; cover about 4" (10 cm) of the metal ring.

2 Curl ribbon tails with blade of scissors. Tie pieces of wrapped candy to wreath; space evenly. Pack knotted ribbons tightly.

3 Repeat steps 1 and 2 until the entire wreath is covered. Fold 40" (102 cm) length of curling ribbon in half; wrap folded end around metal ring at top of wreath. Knot, allowing 2" (5 cm) loop for hanger.

4 Insert tails of ribbon through handle of small scissors; knot, allowing scissors to hang just below wreath. Curl ribbon tails.

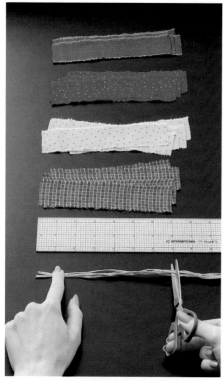

1 Cut selvages from fabrics. Tear fabric crosswise into strips, 1½" (3.8 cm) wide. Cut strips into 7" (18 cm) lengths. Cut raffia into 7" (18 cm) lengths.

2 Wrap length of fabric around metal ring; knot, leaving tails of equal length. Wrap length of raffia around metal ring next to knotted fabric; knot, leaving tails of equal length. Repeat until entire ring is covered, alternating fabrics and packing knots close together.

3 Tie wrapped candies to wreath where desired, using raffia tails.

4 Fold 36" (91.5 cm) length of raffia in half; wrap the folded end around the metal ring at top of wreath. Knot, allowing 2" (5 cm) loop for the hanger. Insert tails of raffia through the handle of a small pair of scissors; knot, allowing the scissors to hang just below wreath.

HOLIDAY COASTER SETS

As a gift for the hostess, make a set of holiday coasters and package them in a decorative box. Purchase a small cardboard box and lid in a holiday-motif shape, such as a star, heart, or tree. Make the padded coasters in the same shape as the box, using cotton quilting fabric and needlepunched cotton batting. Paint the box, and adorn the lid with an additional coaster, giving a clue to the contents of the box.

MATERIALS

- Cardboard box in holiday-motif shape, such as a star, heart, or tree, measuring about 2" (5 cm) high and 4" to 5" (10 to 12.5 cm) in diameter.
- ½ yd. (0.5 m) cotton quilting fabric in Christmas print.

- ½ yd. (0.5 m) needlepunched cotton batting.
- Pinking shears.
- Embellishments, such as tiny buttons or ribbons, optional.
- Acrylic paint and paintbrush.
- Craft glue.

HOW TO MAKE A HOLIDAY COASTER SET

1 Prewash fabric and batting, following the manufacturer's instructions. Fold fabric in half, wrong sides together, matching selvages. Trace the box bottom on right side of fabric eight times, for eight coasters; allow ½" (1.3 cm) between coasters. Trace the box lid once for larger coaster.

2 Insert batting between the layers of fabric. Secure fabric and batting layers together, using two or three pins in each traced coaster.

3 Cut coasters apart through all layers, leaving irregular margins around each coaster. Stitch layers together, using small stitches, and stitching ¼" (6 mm) inside traced lines.

4 Cut out coasters just inside traced lines, using pinking shears. Embellish the coasters with small buttons or other embellishments, if desired.

5 Paint all surfaces of cardboard box and lid, using acrylic paint and paintbrush. Allow to dry.

6 Insert the eight small coasters into box. Embellish large coaster for lid with bow or other embellishment, if desired. Secure large coaster to lid, using craft glue.

PIECED STAR
TABLE TOPPERS

This eight-pointed reversible star adds a decorative touch to tables. Use it as a table topper over a skirted round table. Or drape it over a dining table, sofa table, or end table.

The star is made by stitching eight diamonds together. The outer half of each diamond is cut longer than the inner half, creating extended points that can be draped over the edges of a table. The finished star measures about 50" (127 cm) in diameter. Tassels can be added to the points of the stars for additional embellishment.

The star and the lining can be sewn from a single fabric. Or use two or more fabrics for variety. If more than one fabric is used, become familiar with the piecing technique in order to plan the placement of the pieces before you

begin to stitch. The lining is constructed using the same method as for the star, making the table topper reversible.

MATERIALS

- 3 yd. (2.75 m) fabric, for star and lining from one fabric, or ¾ yd. (0.7 m) each of four fabrics, for star and lining from four fabrics.
- Eight tassels, optional.

CUTTING DIRECTIONS

Make the pattern as on page 142. Cut eight diamonds from the fabric or fabrics for the star. Also cut eight diamonds from the fabric for the lining.

Pieced star table toppers can be made in a variety of styles. Above, the star topper with a country look is made from four different cotton fabrics. Opposite, an elegant star topper is made from a single fabric and embellished with tassels at each of the points.

HOW TO MAKE A PIECED STAR TABLE TOPPER PATTERN

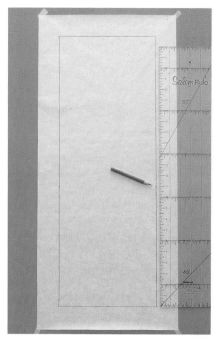 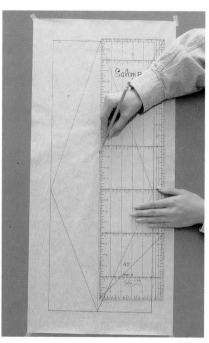 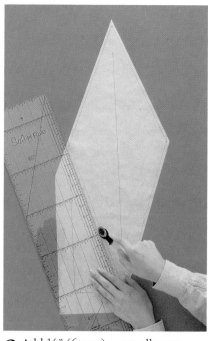

1 Draw 9¼" × 25" (23.6 × 63.5 cm) rectangle on paper. Mark a dot at the center of each short side. Mark a dot along each long side, 11" (28 cm) from one end.

2 Draw lines connecting the dots as shown. Mark grainline parallel to long sides of rectangle.

3 Add ¼" (6 mm) seam allowances to the diamond pattern, outside the marked lines. Cut out pattern.

HOW TO SEW A PIECED STAR TABLE TOPPER

1 Align two of the diamonds, right sides together and raw edges even. Stitch ¼" (6 mm) seam on one short side, stitching toward narrow point. Repeat for remaining pieces to make four 2-diamond units.

2 Stitch two of the 2-diamond units, right sides together, along one short side; finger-press seam allowances in opposite directions as shown. Repeat for the remaining two units.

3 Place the two 4-diamond units right sides together. Pin, matching inner points of diamonds at center. Fold seam allowances of each unit in opposite directions; stitch seam from outer edges toward center.

4 Release the stitching within the seam allowances at center of star, so seam allowances will lie flat. Press from wrong side, working from center out.

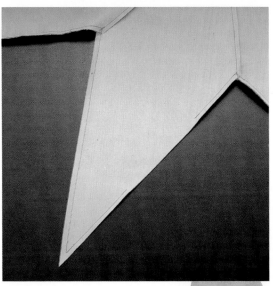

5 Repeat steps 1 to 4 for lining. Pin the star and the lining, right sides together, matching the raw edges and seams; the seam allowances will face in opposite directions. Stitch around star, stitching from inside corners to points; leave 6" (15 cm) opening on one side, for turning.

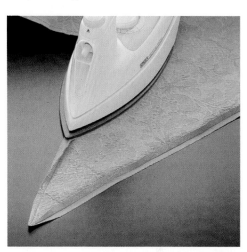

6 Clip inside corners, and trim points. Press the seam allowances open around the outer edges.

7 Turn star right side out; press. Slipstitch opening closed. Stitch a tassel to each point, if desired.

PACKAGE PLACEMATS

Dress up a holiday table with pieced placemats that have the three-dimensional look of wrapped packages. The dimensional illusion is achieved by using fabrics in light, medium, and dark colors. A simple bow, created from a pleated fabric square and a fabric loop, completes the package.

The placemat is made from either lightweight cotton or cotton blends, using quick cutting and piecing techniques for easy construction. The instructions that follow are for a set of four placemats that measure about 13" × 17" (33 × 43 cm). Stitch the placemats using ¼" (6 mm) seam allowances.

MATERIALS (for four placemats)

- ¼ yd. (0.25 m) light-colored fabric, for package top.
- ½ yd. (0.5 m) medium-colored fabric, for package front.
- ¼ yd. (0.25 m) dark-colored fabric, for package side.
- ⅝ yd. (0.6 m) fabric, for ribbon and bow.
- ⅞ yd. (0.8 m) fabric, for backing.
- Low-loft quilt batting.
- Quilter's ruler with an edge at 45° angle.

CUTTING DIRECTIONS

Cut the following strips on the crosswise grain, cutting across the full width of the fabric: two 6½" (16.3 cm) strips from the fabric for the package front; two 2" (5 cm) strips from the fabric for the package side; and four 2" (5 cm) strips from the fabric for the package top. From the fabric for the ribbon and bow, cut: four 1½" (3.8 cm) strips and one 1¼" (3.2 cm) strip, for the ribbon; eight 6½" (16.3 cm) squares, for the bows; and one 2½" × 15" (6.5 × 38 cm) strip, for the loop of the bow. Cut four 13½" × 17½" (34.3 × 44.3 cm) rectangles each from the backing fabric and batting.

HOW TO SEW A SET OF PACKAGE PLACEMATS

1 Stitch package front strips to each side of one 1½" (3.8 cm) ribbon strip, to make pieced strip for package fronts. Press the seam allowances toward ribbon strip. From pieced strip, cut four 9½" × 13½" (24.3 × 34.3 cm) rectangles.

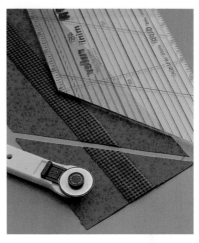

2 Stitch package side strips to each side of one 1½" (3.8 cm) ribbon strip, to make pieced strip for package sides. Press the seam allowances toward ribbon strip. Cut off one end of pieced strip at 45° angle, as shown.

(Continued)

3 Measure and mark strip at 9¾" (25 cm) intervals. Cut four parallelograms for package sides, as shown.

4 Stitch package top strips to each side of one 1½" (3.8 cm) ribbon strip, to make the pieced strip for the package tops. Repeat to make two pieced strips. Press seam allowances toward ribbon strips. Cut off one end of each pieced strip at a 45° angle, as shown; the angle is cut in the opposite direction from the angle of package side strips.

5 Measure and mark the package top strips at 6¾" (17 cm) intervals. Cut into eight parallelograms for package tops.

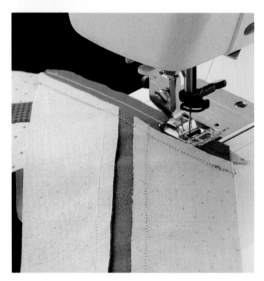

6 Stitch the 1¼" (3.2 cm) ribbon strip to one angled end of one of the parallelograms for package top; allow excess fabric from ribbon strip at each end. Press seam allowances toward ribbon strip; trim strip even with edges of the parallelogram. Stitch second parallelogram for package top to the opposite side of ribbon strip; press the seam allowances toward the ribbon strip. Repeat to make four package tops.

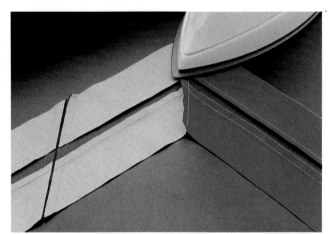

7 Align one package top to one package side along the angled edges, with right sides together and raw edges even. Stitch from sharply pointed end to ¼" (6 mm) from inside corner; backstitch to secure stitching. Press the seam allowances toward package top.

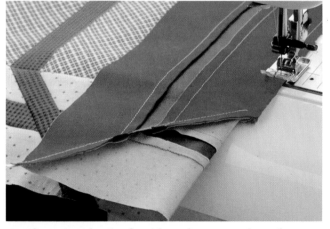

8 Align pieced strips for side and top to package front, matching ribbon strips of top and front. Stitch from outer edges exactly to the seam intersection. Press seam allowances toward top and side.

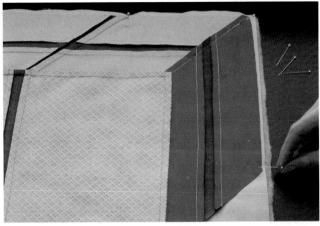

9 Place the backing and placemat top right sides together. Place fabrics on batting, with pieced design on top; pin or baste layers together.

10 Stitch around the placemat top, ¼" (6 mm) from raw edges; leave 4" (10 cm) opening for turning. Trim the excess backing and batting; trim corners.

11 Turn the placemat right side out; press. Slipstitch opening closed. Quilt placemat by stitching on seamlines, using monofilament nylon thread in needle and thread that matches backing fabric in the bobbin. (Contrasting thread was used to show detail.)

12 Fold strip for loop of bow in half lengthwise, right sides together. Stitch ¼" (6 mm) seam; turn tube right side out. Press, with the seam centered on one side. Cut tube into four 3" (7.5 cm) strips.

13 Press raw edges ¼" (6 mm) to inside at one end of each tube; tuck opposite end inside the tube to make a loop. Stitch ends together. Pin loop, as shown, over intersecting ribbons on package top. Slipstitch in place.

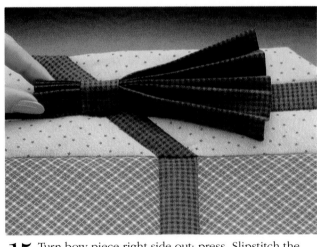

14 Place two fabric pieces for bow right sides together, matching raw edges. Stitch ¼" (6 mm) from raw edges, leaving 2" (5 cm) opening for turning. Trim the corners; press the seams open.

15 Turn bow piece right side out; press. Slipstitch the opening closed. Hand-pleat fabric, and insert into loop for bow.

HOLIDAY PLACEMATS & TABLE RUNNERS

Create a variety of looks for the holiday table using simple stitched-and-turned placemats and table runners. Choose to make placemats and a matching rectangular table runner, or sew a table runner that has pointed ends. Embellish the placemats and table runner with coordinating braid, ribbon, or other flat trims.

The instructions that follow are for placemats with a finished size of 13" × 18" (33 × 46 cm). The length of the table runner is determined by the length of the table and the desired drop length, or overhang, at the ends of the table.

MATERIALS (for four placemats)

- 1⅝ yd. (1.5 m) fabric, for the placemat top and backing pieces.
- 1⅝ yd. (1.5 m) fusible interfacing.
- Braid or other flat trim.

MATERIALS (for table runner)

- Fabric, for table runner top and backing pieces; yardage varies, depending on length of runner.
- Fusible or sew-in interfacing; yardage varies, depending on length of runner.
- Braid or other flat trim.

CUTTING DIRECTIONS

For each placemat, cut two 13½" × 18½" (34.3 × 47.3 cm) rectangles from fabric, for the placemat top and backing. Cut one 13½" × 18½" (34.3 × 47.3 cm) rectangle from fusible interfacing.

For a table runner, cut two rectangles from fabric for the table runner top and backing, and cut one rectangle from fusible interfacing. The width of the rectangles is 18½" (47.3 cm); the length is equal to the length of the table plus two times the desired drop length, plus ½" (1.3 cm) for the seam allowances.

HOW TO SEW A BASIC PLACEMAT OR TABLE RUNNER

1 Apply interfacing to the wrong side of placemat or table runner top; if using fusible interfacing, follow manufacturer's directions.

2 Pin top to backing, right sides together. Stitch around placemat or table runner, ¼" (6 mm) from raw edges; leave 4" (10 cm) opening for turning. Trim corners.

3 Turn the placemat or table runner right side out; press. Slipstitch the opening closed. If desired, embellish with braid trim (page 150).

HOW TO SEW A TABLE RUNNER WITH POINTED ENDS

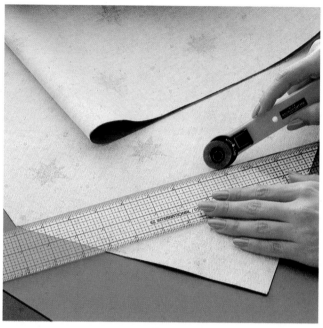

1 Mark the center of one short end on rectangle for table runner top. From same short end, measure distance on each long edge equal to the desired drop length plus ¼" (6 mm) for seam allowance; mark. Draw lines from marking on short end to markings on long edges.

2 Fold rectangle for table runner top in half crosswise; align the raw edges. Cut on marked lines through both layers. Cut backing and interfacing to match table runner top. Complete table runner as on page 149, steps 1 to 3.

HOW TO EMBELLISH A PLACEMAT OR TABLE RUNNER WITH BRAID TRIM

1 Pin braid trim to the placemat or table runner at desired distance from edge; miter the braid trim at corners by folding it at an angle. Fold end of braid diagonally at final corner; trim excess.

2 Edgestitch along inner and outer edges of braid trim; hand-stitch mitered corners in place.

MORE IDEAS FOR THE TABLE

Motifs cut from printed fabric are fused to a solid background to make an interesting table covering. Simply fuse motifs to background fabric, using fusible web; then conceal cut edges of fabric, using acrylic craft paints in fine-tip tubes.

Ribbon, wrapped package-style around a table, creates a holiday atmosphere. Secure the ribbon in place on the underside of the table, using masking tape.

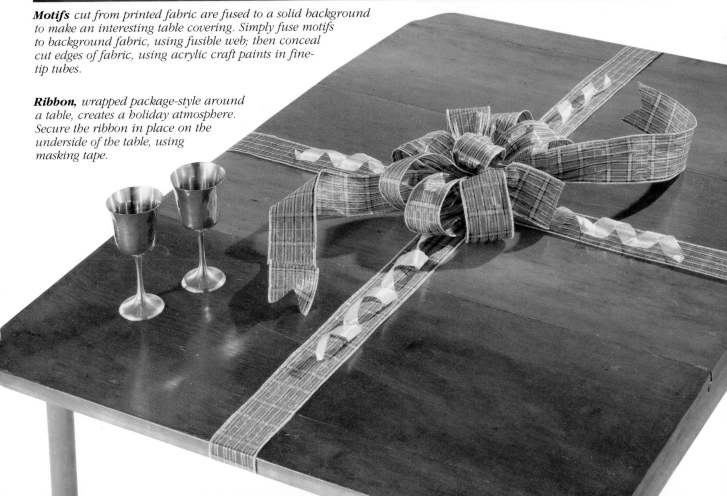

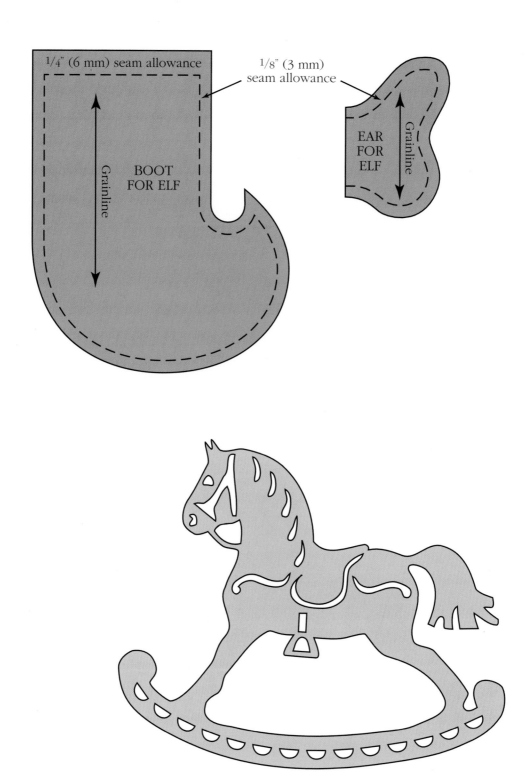

ROCKING HORSE ORNAMENT
Dimensions 3½" × 4¼" (9 × 10.8 cm)

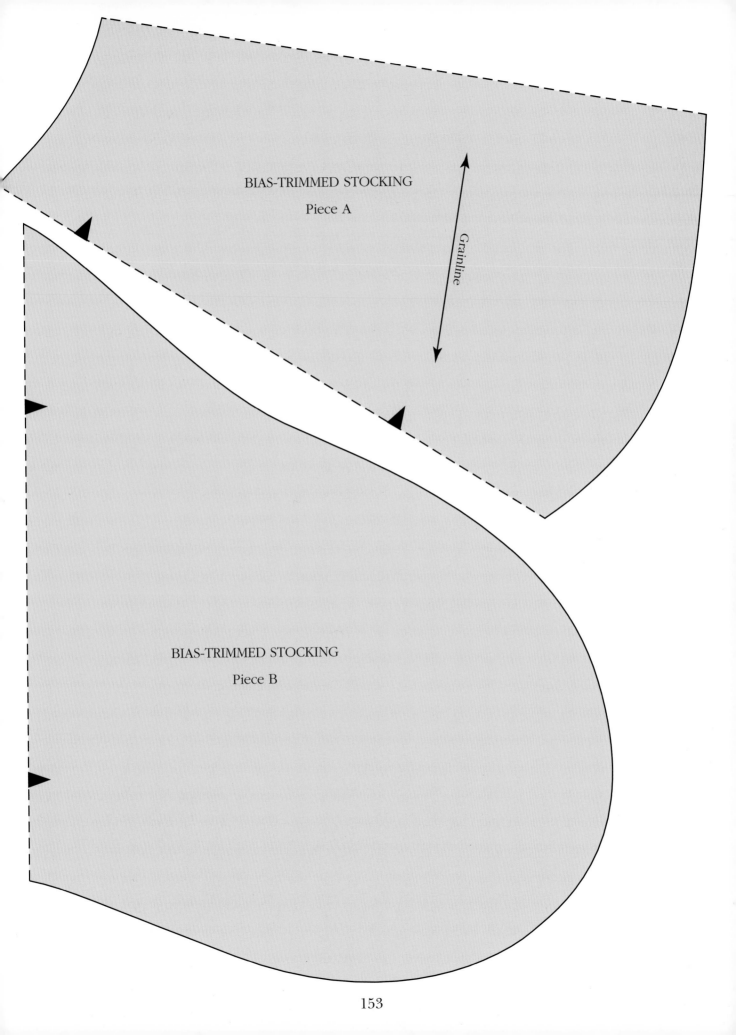

BIAS-TRIMMED STOCKING

Piece A

Grainline

BIAS-TRIMMED STOCKING

Piece B

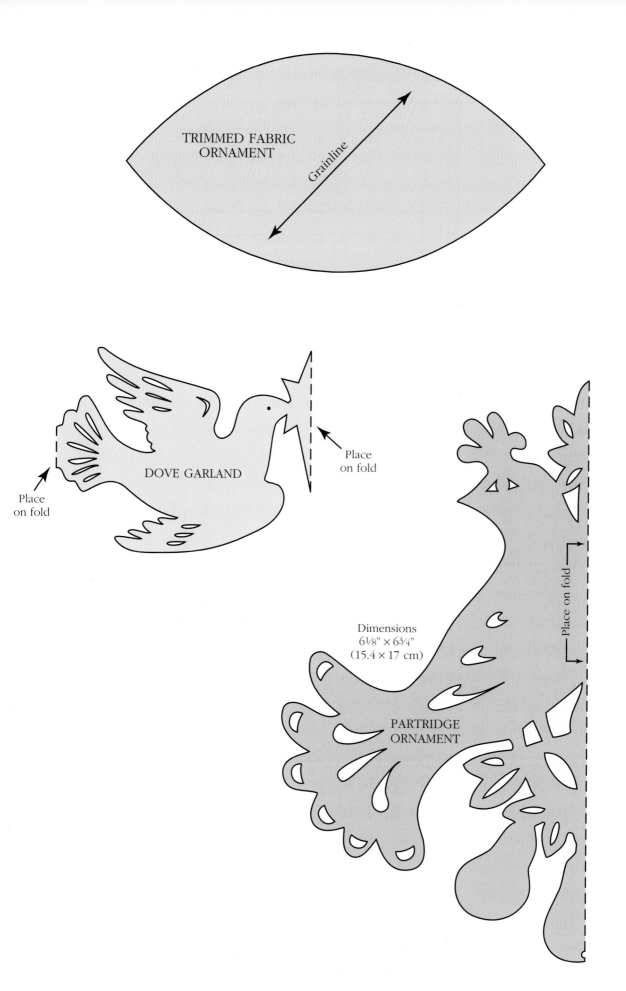

TRIMMED FABRIC
ORNAMENT

Grainline

DOVE GARLAND

Place
on fold

Place
on fold

Dimensions
6⅛" × 6¾"
(15.4 × 17 cm)

Place on fold

PARTRIDGE
ORNAMENT

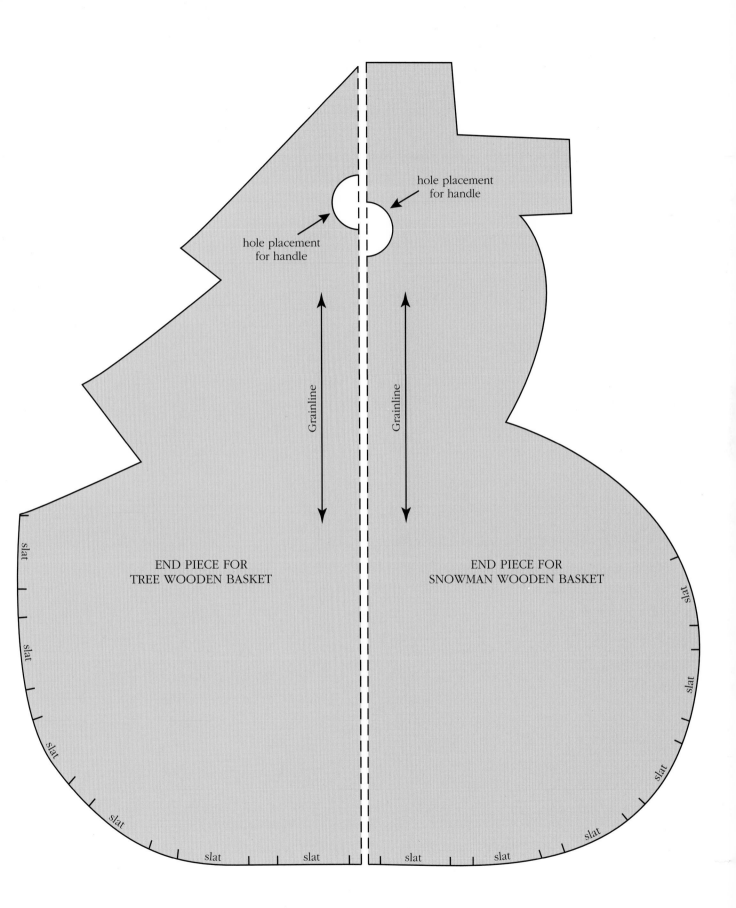

hole placement
for handle

hole placement
for handle

Grainline

Grainline

END PIECE FOR
TREE WOODEN BASKET

END PIECE FOR
SNOWMAN WOODEN BASKET

slat

slat

slat

slat

slat

slat

slat

slat

slat

slat

slat

slat

slat

slat

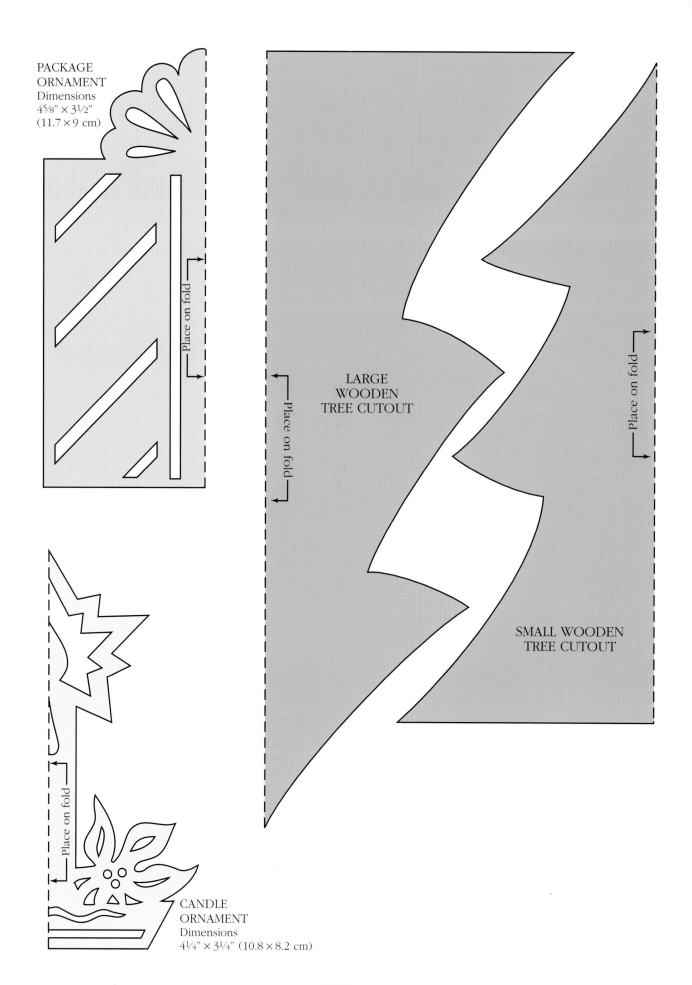

PACKAGE
ORNAMENT
Dimensions
4⅝" × 3½"
(11.7 × 9 cm)

Place on fold

LARGE
WOODEN
TREE CUTOUT

Place on fold

Place on fold

SMALL WOODEN
TREE CUTOUT

Place on fold

CANDLE
ORNAMENT
Dimensions
4¼" × 3¼" (10.8 × 8.2 cm)

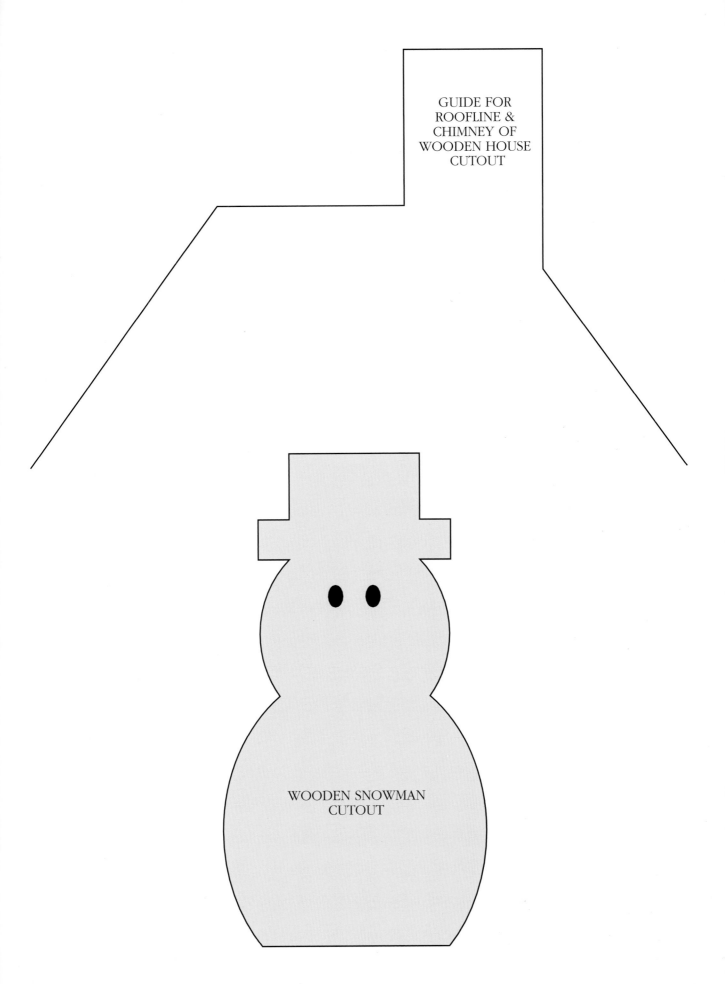

GUIDE FOR
ROOFLINE &
CHIMNEY OF
WOODEN HOUSE
CUTOUT

WOODEN SNOWMAN
CUTOUT

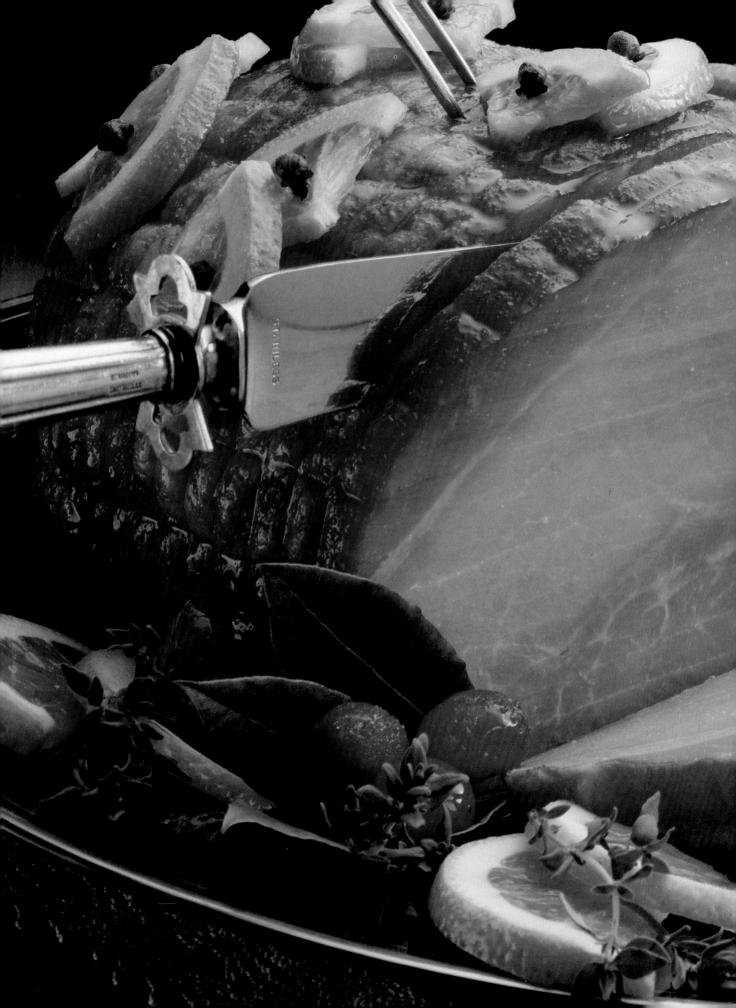

APPETIZERS

SEAFOOD & AVOCADO DIP

- 1 large ripe avocado
- Lemon juice
- 1 pkg. (3 oz./85 g) cream cheese
- 1 tablespoon (15 mL) sliced green onion
- 1 small clove garlic, minced
- ½ cup (125 mL) shredded seafood sticks or rinsed and drained crab meat
- 1 teaspoon (5 mL) lime juice
- ¼ teaspoon (1 mL) Worcestershire sauce
- Pinch cayenne

6 to 8 servings

1 Cut avocado in half lengthwise and remove the pit. With small spoon, scoop out pulp, leaving ¼" (5 mm) shell. Chop avocado pulp and set aside. Brush surfaces of avocado shells with lemon juice. Set aside.

2 In small mixing bowl, place cream cheese, green onion and garlic. Microwave at High for 15 to 30 seconds, or until cheese softens. Mix in chopped avocado pulp and remaining ingredients. Stuff seafood mixture evenly into avocado shells. Place one shell on plate. Microwave at High for 30 seconds to 1 minute, or until dip is warm. Repeat with second avocado shell if needed. Serve dip with corn or tortilla chips, or assorted crackers.

TIP: *Dip is conveniently served in its own natural container. Microwave one avocado shell, and refrigerate second shell until more warm dip is needed.*

LAYERED BEAN DIP

Garbanzo Bean Layer:

- 1 can (15 oz./426 mL) garbanzo beans, rinsed and drained
- 1 to 2 tablespoons (15 to 25 mL) fresh lemon juice
- 1 tablespoon (15 mL) olive oil
- 2 cloves garlic, minced
- ½ teaspoon (2 mL) ground cumin
- ¼ teaspoon (1 mL) salt

Black Bean Layer:

- 1 can (15 oz./426 mL) black beans, rinsed and drained
- ½ cup (125 mL) chopped freshly roasted red pepper or roasted red peppers in marinade, rinsed and drained
- 1 tablespoon (15 mL) snipped fresh cilantro
- 1 tablespoon (15 mL) finely chopped green onion

Yogurt Layer:

- 1 cup (250 mL) nonfat yogurt cheese
- 1 to 2 tablespoons (15 to 25 mL) snipped fresh cilantro
- 2 to 3 teaspoons (10 to 15 mL) snipped fresh mint leaves
- 1 to 2 teaspoons (5 to 10 mL) fresh lemon juice

- 1 cup (250 mL) finely shredded lettuce
- 1 Roma tomato, chopped
- 1 tablespoon (15 mL) chopped black or Kalamata olives (optional)

12 servings

1 Combine garbanzo bean layer ingredients in food processor or blender. Process until smooth. Spread the mixture evenly in bottom of 9" (23 cm) pie plate. Set aside.

2 Combine black bean layer ingredients in medium mixing bowl. Spread mixture evenly over garbanzo bean layer to within 1" (2.5 cm) of edge. In small mixing bowl, combine yogurt layer ingredients. Spoon yogurt mixture evenly over black bean layer. Cover with plastic wrap. Chill at least 1 hour.

3 Arrange lettuce and tomato around edges of dip. Garnish with olives. Serve dip with chips, pita bread or raw vegetable sticks, if desired.

TIP: To roast fresh peppers, first pierce the skin several times with a fork. If roasting over a gas burner, spear pepper with long-handled fork and hold over flame, turning until skin is blackened. If using a broiler, place peppers on broiler pan as close to heat as possible, turning until skin is blackened. Place peppers in closed paper bag for about 10 minutes; then peel and use.

HOT & SPICY CHICKEN WINGS

- 3 lbs. (1.36 kg) chicken wings (approximately 15 wings), skin removed

Marinade:

- 1 cup (250 mL) white vinegar, divided
- 2 red chili peppers, seeded and finely chopped
- ½ cup (125 mL) packed brown sugar
- ¼ cup (50 mL) honey
- 2 cloves garlic, minced
- 2 teaspoons (10 mL) cayenne
- 1 teaspoon (5 mL) salt

- Celery sticks (optional)
- Fat-free blue cheese dressing (optional)

5 servings

1 Cut off and discard wing tips from chicken (or save for making stock). Cut each wing at joint to make 2 pieces. Set aside.

2 Combine ¼ cup (50 mL) vinegar and the chili peppers in blender. Process until almost smooth. In large plastic food-storage bag, combine pepper mixture, remaining ¾ cup (175 mL) vinegar and remaining marinade ingredients. Add chicken. Seal bag. Turn bag to coat chicken. Refrigerate at least 6 hours or overnight, turning bag occasionally.

3 Heat oven to 400°F/200°C. Drain marinade from meat into 2-qt. (2 L) saucepan. Set wings aside. Bring marinade to a boil over medium-high heat. Reduce heat to medium. Boil for 12 to 20 minutes, or until sauce is reduced by half, stirring occasionally. Remove from heat. Set aside.

4 Line baking sheet with foil. Spray wire rack with nonstick vegetable cooking spray. Place rack on prepared sheet. Arrange wings on rack. Brush wings generously with sauce.

5 Bake for 20 minutes. Turn wings over. Brush again. Bake for 10 minutes. Brush again. Bake for additional 5 to 10 minutes, or until wings are deep golden brown. Serve wings with any remaining sauce, the celery and dressing.

TIP: *For spicier wings, include chili pepper seeds in marinade.*

162

SUN-DRIED TOMATO & GARLIC SPREAD

- 1 whole bulb garlic
- 1 cup (250 mL) boiling water
- 2 oz. (60 g) dry-pack sun-dried tomatoes (about 1 cup/250 mL)
- 2 tablespoons (25 mL) pine nuts, toasted*
- 2 tablespoons (25 mL) shredded fresh Parmesan cheese
- 2 teaspoons (10 mL) snipped fresh basil leaves
- 1 fresh baguette (8 oz./250 g), cut into 24 slices, toasted

8 servings

To toast pine nuts, cook in a dry skillet over medium-low heat, stirring frequently to prevent burning.

1 Heat oven to 350°F/180°C. Remove outer peel of garlic bulb without separating cloves. Cut off and discard top 1/3 of each clove. Place garlic in center of 12" x 9" (30 x 23 cm) sheet of foil. Fold opposite edges of foil together, crimping edges to seal. Place foil packet on rack in oven. Bake for 1 hour. Let packet stand 10 to 15 minutes, or until garlic is cool enough to handle. Squeeze soft garlic from each clove peel. Set roasted garlic aside.

2 Meanwhile, in small mixing bowl, combine water and tomatoes. Let stand 30 minutes. Drain, reserving liquid. In food processor or blender, combine tomatoes, roasted garlic, pine nuts, Parmesan cheese and basil. Process until smooth, adding enough of reserved liquid to make smooth spread. Transfer spread to small mixing bowl. Cover with plastic wrap. Refrigerate overnight to blend flavors. To serve, spread tomato and garlic spread evenly on toast slices.

TOMATO & FETA PITA PIZZAS

- 3 Roma tomatoes, finely chopped
- 1 tablespoon (15 mL) crumbled feta cheese
- 1 green onion, finely chopped
- 2 teaspoons (10 mL) balsamic vinegar
- 1 teaspoon (5 mL) olive oil
- ¼ teaspoon (1 mL) dried oregano leaves
- ¼ teaspoon (1 mL) pepper
- 4 whole soft pitas

8 servings

1 Combine all ingredients, except pitas, in small mixing bowl. Cover with plastic wrap. Let stand 20 minutes.

2 Heat oven to 350°F/180°C. Arrange pitas on baking sheet. Spread tomato mixture evenly over pitas. Bake for 10 to 12 minutes, or until hot. Cut each pita into 4 wedges to serve.

TIP: *These pizzas can also be served as a main dish.*

BBQ CHICKEN PITA PIZZAS

- 1 cup (250 mL) cubed cooked chicken breast (no skin; ½"/1 cm cubes)
- ¼ cup (50 mL) prepared barbecue sauce
- 4 whole soft pitas
- ¼ cup (50 mL) shredded reduced-fat Cheddar cheese

8 servings

1 Heat oven to 350°F/180°C. In small mixing bowl, combine chicken and barbecue sauce. Set aside.

2 Arrange pitas on baking sheet. Spread chicken mixture evenly over pitas. Sprinkle cheese evenly over top. Bake for 10 to 12 minutes, or until pitas are hot and cheese is melted.

- ½ cup (125 mL) ready-to-serve chicken broth, divided
- 1 large onion, sliced into ¼" (5 mm) rings
- 4 whole soft pitas
- 4 teaspoons (20 mL) shredded fresh Parmesan cheese
- 1 teaspoon (5 mL) snipped fresh rosemary leaves

8 servings

1 Heat ¼ cup (50 mL) broth in 10" (25 cm) nonstick skillet over medium-low heat until bubbly. Add onion. Cook for 35 to 40 minutes, or until onion is dark golden brown, stirring occasionally. Sprinkle only enough of remaining ¼ cup (50 mL) broth over onion as needed to prevent burning. (Adding too much broth at one time will make onions soggy and prevent browning.)

2 Heat oven to 350°F/180°C. Arrange pitas on baking sheet. Spread onion evenly over pitas. Sprinkle cheese and rosemary evenly over top. Bake for 10 to 12 minutes, or until pitas are hot and cheese is melted.

ANTIPASTO KABOBS

- 1 pkg. (9 oz./255 g) fresh cheese tortelloni or ravioli
- 1 can (14 oz./398 mL) quartered artichoke hearts in water, rinsed and drained
- 1 small red pepper, seeded and cut into 40 chunks
- 20 small fresh mushrooms, cut in half
- 10 jumbo pitted black olives, cut in half
- 10 large pimiento-stuffed green olives, cut in half
- 20 wooden skewers (10"/25 cm)
- 1 bottle (16 oz./500 mL) fat-free Italian dressing

20 kabobs

1 Prepare tortelloni as directed on package. Rinse with cold water. Drain.

2 Cut large artichoke heart quarters in half lengthwise in order to get 20 pieces. Thread ingredients on skewers as follows: pepper chunk, mushroom half, tortelloni, black olive half, artichoke heart, green olive half, tortelloni, mushroom half and pepper chunk.

3 Arrange kabobs in a shallow dish. Pour dressing evenly over kabobs, turning to coat. Cover. Chill at least 2 hours, turning kabobs occasionally. Drain dressing from kabobs before serving.

TIP: *Drained dressing may be reserved for other uses.*

BREAKFAST FARE

SEAFOOD & LEEK TART

Pastry:
- 1¼ cups (300 mL) all-purpose flour
- Pinch salt
- ½ cup (125 mL) butter or margarine
- 3 to 4 tablespoons (50 mL) cold water

Filling:
- 1 tablespoon (15 mL) butter or margarine
- 2 cups (6 oz./170 g) sliced fresh mushrooms
- ½ cup (125 mL) sliced leeks or chopped onion
- 1 cup (250 mL) half-and-half
- 8 oz. (250 g) frozen tiny salad shrimp or cooked crab, thawed, well drained
- 2 egg yolks, slightly beaten
- ½ teaspoon (2 mL) salt
- ¼ teaspoon (1 mL) pepper
- ⅛ to ¼ teaspoon (0.5 to 1 mL) hot pepper sauce

8 servings

1 Heat oven to 400°F/200°C. In small bowl, combine flour and pinch of salt. Cut in ½ cup (125 mL) butter until crumbly; with fork, mix in water until dough clings together. Form into ball. On lightly floured surface, roll pastry into 14" (35.5 cm) circle. Place in greased 12" (30 cm) tart pan; press into and against sides of pan. Cut away excess pastry; prick with fork. Bake for 12 to 14 minutes, or until lightly browned.

2 Meanwhile, in 10" (25 cm) skillet, melt 1 tablespoon (15 mL) butter. Add mushrooms and leeks. Cook over medium heat, until vegetables are tender (4 to 5 minutes). Remove from heat.

3 In small bowl, stir together half-and-half, shrimp, egg yolks, salt, pepper and hot pepper sauce. Stir into mushroom mixture. Pour into baked pastry shells. Bake for 18 to 22 minutes, or until set and golden brown.

BLUEBERRY MUFFINS

- ½ cup (125 mL) sugar
- ¼ cup (50 mL) butter or margarine, softened
- 1 cup (250 mL) sour cream
- 2 tablespoons (25 mL) frozen orange juice concentrate, defrosted
- 2 teaspoons (10 mL) grated lemon peel
- 1 egg
- 1½ cups (375 mL) all-purpose flour
- 1 teaspoon (5 mL) baking soda
- 1 cup (250 mL) fresh or frozen blueberries (unthawed)
- 1 tablespoon (15 mL) sugar
- ½ teaspoon (2 mL) grated lemon peel

1 dozen

1 Heat oven to 375°F/190°C. In large mixer bowl, combine ½ cup (125 mL) sugar and the butter. Beat at medium speed, scraping bowl often, until well mixed (1 to 2 minutes). Add sour cream, orange juice concentrate, 2 teaspoons (10 mL) peel and the egg. Continue beating, scraping bowl often, until well mixed (1 to 2 minutes).

2 In medium bowl, stir together flour and baking soda. By hand, stir flour mixture into sour cream mixture just until moistened. Fold in blueberries. Spoon into greased muffin pan.

3 In small bowl, stir together 1 tablespoon (15 mL) sugar and ½ teaspoon (2 mL) peel. Sprinkle about ¼ teaspoon (1 mL) mixture on top of each muffin. Bake for 20 to 25 minutes, or until lightly browned. Cool 5 minutes; remove from pan.

TIPSY FRUIT PARFAITS

- ½ cup (125 mL) sour cream
- 2 teaspoons (10 mL) orange-flavored liqueur, optional
- 1 teaspoon (5 mL) grated orange peel
- 3 cups (750 mL) cut-up fruit (seedless grapes, mandarin orange segments, pineapple, kiwi, strawberries, blueberries, etc.)
- 3 tablespoons (50 mL) firmly packed brown sugar

4 servings

1 In small bowl, stir together sour cream, liqueur and peel. Up to 1 hour before serving, place about ⅓ cup (75 mL) fruit in bottom of four tall parfait glasses; top each with 1 tablespoon (15 mL) sour cream mixture and about 1 teaspoon (5 mL) brown sugar.

2 Repeat layering one more time, finishing with sour cream mixture and brown sugar. Refrigerate until ready to serve.

HAM & VEGETABLE STRATA

- 12 slices white bread
- 8 ounces (250 g) sharp Cheddar cheese or Swiss cheese, shredded
- 3 cups (750 mL) frozen mixed vegetables
- 1½ cups (375 mL) chopped cooked ham or Canadian bacon
- 3 cups (750 mL) milk
- 6 eggs
- 1½ teaspoons (7 mL) dry mustard
- 2 teaspoons (10 mL) onion powder
- ½ teaspoon (2 mL) salt
- ¼ to ½ teaspoon (1 to 2 mL) cayenne

12 servings

1 With 3" (7.5 cm) cookie cutter, cut a design out of each bread slice; set aside. Tear remaining bread into pieces; place in bottom of greased 13" × 9" (3.5 L) baking pan. Layer with cheese, vegetables, ham and bread cutouts.

2 In medium bowl, beat together all remaining ingredients. Pour evenly over mixture in pan. Cover with plastic wrap; refrigerate 8 hours or overnight.

3 Heat oven to 350°F/180°C. Uncover; bake for 60 to 75 minutes, or until set and golden brown. If browning too quickly, loosely cover with aluminum foil. Let stand for 15 minutes.

BAKED FRUIT AMBROSIA

- 2 large oranges or ruby red grapefruit
- 1 cup (250 mL) fresh pineapple chunks*
- 3 tablespoons (50 mL) firmly packed brown sugar
- 1 tablespoon (15 mL) honey
- 2 tablespoons (25 mL) flaked coconut
- Pomegranate seeds or maraschino cherries

4 servings

1 Heat oven to 350°F/180°C. Cut oranges in half crosswise. With small serrated knife and grapefruit spoon, remove fruit, keeping peel intact. Separate orange sections. In medium bowl, toss together orange sections, pineapple, brown sugar and honey. Spoon into orange cups.

2 Place filled cups in 9" (2.5 L) square baking pan. Bake for 15 minutes. Sprinkle with coconut. Continue baking for 5 to 10 minutes, or until fruit is heated through and coconut is lightly browned. Sprinkle with pomegranate seeds or top each with a maraschino cherry.

*1 (8 oz./250 g) can pineapple chunks, drained, can be substituted for 1 cup (250 mL) fresh pineapple chunks.

TIP: If desired, bake ambrosia in custard cups instead of the orange cups.

LEMON-SCENTED KOLACHI

- 1 pkg. (¼ oz./7 g) active dry yeast
- ¼ cup (50 mL) warm water (105° to 115°F/42° to 47°C)
- 3½ cups (875 mL) all-purpose flour
- ½ teaspoon (2 mL) salt
- 1 cup (250 mL) butter or margarine, softened
- 1 cup (250 mL) half-and-half
- 2 eggs, slightly beaten
- 1 teaspoon (5 mL) grated lemon peel
- 1 jar (10 oz./284 mL) fruit preserves or 1 cup (250 mL) poppy seed filling

2½ dozen kolachi

1 In small bowl, dissolve yeast in warm water. In large bowl, combine flour and salt; cut in butter until crumbly. Stir in yeast, half-and-half, eggs and peel.

2 Turn dough onto lightly floured surface; knead until smooth (2 to 3 minutes). Place in greased bowl, turning to coat. Cover; refrigerate until firm (6 hours or overnight).

3 Heat oven to 375°F/190°C. Roll out dough, ¼ at a time, on sugared surface to ⅛" (3 mm) thickness. Cut into 3" (7.5 cm) squares. Spoon 1 teaspoon (5 mL) preserves in center of each square.

4 Bring up two opposite corners to center; pinch firmly together to seal.

5 Place 1" (2.5 cm) apart on cookie sheets. Bake for 10 to 15 minutes or until lightly browned.

TENDER SOUR CREAM PANCAKES

- 3 eggs, separated
- 1½ cups (375 mL) all-purpose flour
- ¼ cup (50 mL) sugar
- ¼ cup (50 mL) butter or margarine, melted
- 2 cups (500 mL) low-fat sour cream

- 1 to 2 tablespoons (15 to 25 mL) milk
- 2 teaspoons (10 mL) baking powder
- 1 teaspoon (5 mL) baking soda
- ¼ teaspoon (1 mL) salt

18 pancakes

1 In small mixer bowl, beat egg whites at high speed, scraping bowl often, until stiff peaks form (1 to 2 minutes); set aside. In large mixer bowl, combine egg yolks and all remaining ingredients. (Add enough milk for desired consistency.) Beat at medium speed until well mixed. By hand, fold in beaten egg whites. (Small fluffs of egg white will remain in batter.) *

2 Heat griddle to 350°F/180°C, or until drops of water sizzle. For each pancake, pour ¼ cup (50 mL) batter onto greased griddle. Cook until bubbles form (about 1½ minutes). Turn; continue cooking, until underside is light brown (about 1½ minutes). Serve warm.

Blueberry Pancakes: *Prepare as directed to * above. Fold 1 cup (250 mL) fresh or frozen blueberries into pancake batter. Continue as directed.*

Pecan Pancakes: *Prepare as directed to * above. Fold ⅓ cup (75 mL) chopped pecans into pancake batter. Continue as directed.*

Banana-Nut Pancakes: *Prepare as directed to * above. Fold ½ cup (125 mL) mashed banana and ⅓ cup (75 mL) chopped walnuts into pancake batter. Continue as directed.*

CHEESE & MUSHROOM OVEN OMELET

- 1 tablespoon (5 mL) butter or margarine
- 2 cups (6 oz./170 g) sliced fresh mushrooms*
- 6 eggs
- ⅓ cup (75 mL) milk
- 2 tablespoons (25 mL) all-purpose flour

- Pinch pepper
- 1½ cups (6 oz./375 mL) shredded Swiss or Cheddar cheese, divided
- ¼ cup (50 mL) finely chopped Canadian bacon (6 slices)
- ¼ cup (50 mL) finely chopped onion

6 servings

1 Heat oven to 350°F/180°C. In 10" (25 cm) skillet, melt butter; add mushrooms. Cook over medium heat, stirring occasionally, until mushrooms are tender (4 to 6 minutes); drain. Set aside.

2 In medium bowl, combine eggs, milk, flour and pepper. Beat with wire whisk or fork until frothy. Stir in 1 cup (250 mL) cheese, the bacon, onion and mushrooms.

3 Pour into buttered 9" (2.5 mL) square baking pan. Sprinkle with remaining cheese. Bake for 20 to 25 minutes, or until eggs are set in center.

1 can (4 oz./113 g) sliced mushrooms, drained, can be substituted for 6 oz. (170 g) sliced fresh mushrooms.

FRENCH TOAST CROISSANTS

Orange Butter:

- ¼ cup (50 mL) butter or margarine, softened
- 1 tablespoon (15 mL) honey
- ½ teaspoon (2 mL) grated orange peel

French Toast:

- ⅓ cup (75 mL) milk
- 2 eggs, slightly beaten
- 1 tablespoon (15 mL) frozen orange juice concentrate, defrosted
- 4 plain croissants, cut in half crosswise or 8 slices (1"/2.5 cm each) French bread
- Powdered sugar

1 In small mixer bowl, beat together all orange butter ingredients at medium speed, scraping bowl often, until light and fluffy (1 to 2 minutes); set aside. In pie pan, stir together milk, eggs, and orange juice concentrate. Heat 10" (25 cm) nonstick skillet or griddle over medium heat. Spray skillet with nonstick vegetable cooking spray. Dip 4 croissant halves into egg mixture, turning to coat both sides. Place croissant halves, cut side down, in skillet.

2 Cook, turning once, until golden brown (3 to 4 minutes on each side). Remove to serving platter; keep warm. Repeat with remaining 2 tablespoons (25 mL) butter and 4 croissant halves. Dust croissant halves with powdered sugar; serve with orange butter.

4 servings

GINGER PEAR BAKED PANCAKE

Pancake:

- ¼ cup (50 mL) butter or margarine
- 1 cup (250 mL) all-purpose flour
- 2 cups (500 mL) milk
- 3 eggs
- ½ teaspoon (2 mL) salt

Filling:

- 2 tablespoons (25 mL) butter or margarine
- 2 teaspoons (10 mL) cornstarch
- 1 tablespoon (15 mL) cold water
- ⅓ cup (75 mL) firmly packed brown sugar
- ½ teaspoon (2 mL) ground ginger
- ¼ teaspoon (1 mL) ground cinnamon
- 2 medium red pears, cored, sliced ½" (1 cm) thick
- ½ cup (125 mL) golden raisins (optional)

6 servings

1 Heat oven to 400°F/200°C. In 12" × 18" (30 × 46 cm) baking pan, melt ¼ cup (50 mL) butter in oven (5 to 6 minutes). In small mixer bowl, combine all remaining pancake ingredients. Beat at low speed, scraping bowl often, until well mixed (1 or 2 minutes). Pour melted butter into batter; continue beating until well mixed (1 to 2 minutes). Pour batter into hot pan. Bake for 30 to 40 minutes, or until puffed, set in center and golden brown.

2 Meanwhile, in 10" (25 cm) skillet, melt 2 tablespoons (25 mL) butter. In small bowl, stir together cornstarch and water. Stir brown sugar, ginger, cinnamon and cornstarch mixture into butter. Cook over medium heat, stirring constantly, until sugar dissolves and mixture bubbles and thickens (2 or 3 minutes). Stir in pears and raisins. Continue cooking, stirring constantly, until pears are evenly coated and crisply tender (10 to 12 minutes). Spoon filling over hot pancake; serve immediately.

BANANA-CHOCOLATE CHIP MUFFINS ↑

- ¾ cup (175 mL) firmly packed brown sugar
- ½ cup (125 mL) butter or margarine, softened
- 1½ cups (375 mL) mashed ripe bananas
- 2 eggs
- 1 teaspoon (5 mL) vanilla
- 1 teaspoon (5 mL) grated orange peel
- 2 cups (500 mL) all-purpose flour
- 1 teaspoon (5 mL) baking soda
- ¼ teaspoon (1 mL) salt
- ½ cup (125 mL) miniature semisweet chocolate chips

1½ dozen muffins

1 Heat oven to 350°F/180°C. In large mixer bowl, combine brown sugar and butter. Beat at medium speed, scraping bowl often, until mixture is creamy (1 to 2 minutes). Add bananas, eggs, vanilla and peel. Continue beating, scraping bowl often, until well mixed (1 to 2 minutes).

2 In medium bowl, stir together flour, baking soda and salt. Add flour mixture to banana mixture; stir just until moistened. Fold in chocolate chips. Spoon into greased muffin pans. Bake for 18 to 25 minutes, or until light golden brown. Cool 5 minutes; remove from pans.

PEAR CHEESE COFFEE CAKE ↑

Coffee Cake:

- 1½ cups (375 mL) all-purpose flour
- ½ cup (125 mL) sugar
- ½ cup (125 mL) milk
- 1 egg, slightly beaten
- 2 tablespoons (25 mL) butter or margarine, melted
- 2 teaspoons (10 mL) baking powder
- ½ teaspoon (2 mL) salt
- 1 cup (250 mL) shredded sharp Cheddar cheese
- 1 cup (250 mL) chopped pear

Topping:

- ½ cup (125 mL) all-purpose flour
- ⅓ cup (75 mL) firmly packed brown sugar
- ½ teaspoon (2 mL) ground cinnamon
- ½ teaspoon (2 mL) ground ginger
- ¼ cup (50 mL) butter or margarine, melted

9 servings

1 Heat oven to 375°F/190°C. In small mixer bowl, combine all coffee cake ingredients, except cheese and pear. Beat at low speed, scraping bowl often, until well mixed (1 to 2 minutes). By hand, stir in cheese and pear. Spread into greased 9" (23 cm) square baking pan.

2 In small bowl, combine ½ cup (125 mL) flour, the brown sugar, cinnamon and ginger. Stir in butter until crumbly; sprinkle over coffee cake batter. Bake for 25 to 35 minutes, or until wooden pick inserted in center comes out clean.

174

← PEACH CREAM COFFEE CAKE

Coffee Cake:

- 1¾ cups (425 mL) all-purpose flour
- ¾ cup (175 mL) butter or margarine, softened
- ½ cup (125 mL) sugar
- 2 eggs
- 1 teaspoon (5 mL) vanilla
- ½ teaspoon (2 mL) baking powder
- ½ teaspoon (2 mL) baking soda
- ¼ teaspoon (1 mL) salt

Filling:

- 8 oz. (250 g) cream cheese, softened
- ¼ cup (50 mL) sugar
- 1 egg
- 1 teaspoon (5 mL) grated orange peel
- 1 jar (10 oz./284 g) peach preserves

Glaze:

- ⅓ cup (75 mL) powdered sugar
- 2 to 3 teaspoons (10 to 15 mL) orange juice

16 servings

1 Heat oven to 350°F/180°C. Grease and flour bottom and sides of 10" (25 cm) springform pan. In large mixer bowl, combine all coffee cake ingredients. Beat at medium speed, scraping bowl often, until well mixed (1 to 2 minutes). Spread batter over bottom and 2" (5 cm) up sides of prepared pan.

2 In small mixer bowl, combine all filling ingredients, except apricot preserves. Beat at medium speed, scraping bowl often, until smooth (2 to 3 minutes). Pour over batter in pan. Spoon preserves evenly over filling. Bake for 45 to 55 minutes, or until crust is golden brown. Cool 20 minutes; remove sides of pan.

3 Meanwhile, in small bowl, stir together powdered sugar and orange juice until smooth. Drizzle over warm coffee cake. Serve warm or cold; store refrigerated.

HONEY-GLAZED CRANBERRY ↑ CORNMEAL MUFFINS

- 1 cup (250 mL) all-purpose flour
- 1 cup (250 mL) yellow cornmeal
- 2 teaspoons (10 mL) baking powder
- ¼ teaspoon (1 mL) ground allspice
- Pinch salt
- ¾ cup (175 mL) low-fat or nonfat buttermilk
- 1 egg, beaten
- ¼ cup (50 mL) honey
- 2 tablespoons (25 mL) vegetable oil
- 1 teaspoon (5 mL) grated orange peel
- ½ cup (125 mL) chopped fresh or frozen cranberries*

Glaze:

- ¼ cup (50 mL) powdered sugar
- 1 tablespoon (15 mL) honey
- 1 tablespoon (15 mL) water

1 dozen muffins

1 Heat oven to 400°F/200°C. Spray 12 muffin cups with nonstick vegetable cooking spray, or line cups with paper liners. Set aside.

2 Combine flour, cornmeal, baking powder, allspice and salt in large mixing bowl. Add buttermilk, egg, honey, oil and peel. Stir just until dry ingredients are moistened. Fold in cranberries.

3 Spoon batter evenly into prepared muffin cups. Bake for 13 to 15 minutes, or until lightly browned. Loosen muffins from rim of pan. Place on cooling rack.

4 Combine glaze ingredients in small mixing bowl. Drizzle over warm muffins. Serve warm.

If desired, substitute dried cranberries or raisins for fresh cranberries.

175

CARAMEL ROLLS

- 1 pkg. (16 oz./454 g) hot roll mix
- 1 cup (250 mL) hot water (120° to 130°F/45° to 55°C)
- ¼ cup plus 2 tablespoons (60 mL) margarine, softened, divided
- ¼ cup (50 mL) plain nonfat or low-fat yogurt
- ⅔ cup (150 mL) packed brown sugar
- ¼ cup (50 mL) light corn syrup
- ¼ cup (50 mL) granulated sugar
- 2 teaspoons (10 mL) ground cinnamon

12 servings

1 Combine hot roll mix, water, 1 tablespoon (15 mL) margarine and the yogurt in large mixing bowl. Stir until dough pulls away from side of bowl. Turn dough out onto lightly floured surface. Knead for 5 to 8 minutes, or until smooth and elastic, adding additional flour as needed to reduce stickiness. Cover dough with bowl. Let rest for 5 minutes.

2 Meanwhile, spray 13" × 9" (3.5 L) baking pan with nonstick vegetable cooking spray. Set aside. In 1-qt. (1 L) saucepan, combine ¼ cup (50 mL) margarine, the brown sugar and corn syrup. Cook over medium-low heat for 2 to 4 minutes, or just until margarine is melted, stirring constantly. Pour caramel into prepared pan, spreading to coat bottom. Set aside.

3 Combine granulated sugar and cinnamon in small bowl. Set aside. On lightly floured surface, roll dough into 15" × 12" (38 × 30.5 cm) rectangle. Spread remaining 1 tablespoon (15 mL) margarine evenly over dough to within ½" (1 cm) of edge. Sprinkle cinnamon mixture evenly over margarine. Starting with short end, roll up dough, jelly roll style. Pinch long edge to seal.

4 Cut roll crosswise into 12 pieces. Arrange pieces evenly spaced over caramel. Cover with light cloth. Let rise in warm place for 30 to 35 minutes, or until rolls are nearly doubled in size. Heat oven to 375°F/190°C. Uncover rolls. Bake for 30 to 35 minutes, or until rolls are golden brown. To serve, invert rolls on serving plate. Serve warm.

TIP: *Using thread to cut roll into pieces will keep the pieces round. Slide 12" (30.5 cm) piece of thread underneath roll. Cross ends of thread over top of roll to form a loop. Pull crossed ends away from each other to tighten loop and cut through roll.*

DENVER OMELET SANDWICHES

- 4 eggs, beaten
- ¼ cup (50 mL) cubed fully cooked ham (¼"/6 mm cubes)
- ¼ cup (50 mL) finely chopped green pepper
- ¼ cup (50 mL) finely chopped onion
- Pinch pepper
- Dash red pepper sauce
- 4 bagels, split in half and toasted; or 8 slices whole wheat bread, toasted
- 4 slices (¾ oz./21 g each) pasteurized process cheese product (optional)
- 4 slices tomato
- Lettuce leaves

1 Combine eggs, ham, green pepper, onion, pepper and red pepper sauce in small mixing bowl. Set aside. Spray 7" (18 cm) nonstick skillet with nonstick vegetable cooking spray. Heat skillet over medium-low heat. Pour ⅓ cup (75 mL) egg mixture into skillet, tilting skillet to coat bottom. Cook for 3½ to 6 minutes, or until omelet is set and bottom is lightly browned. Remove from heat.

2 Fold omelet in half, then in half again. Place omelet on 1 bagel half. Place 1 slice cheese, 1 slice tomato and lettuce over omelet. Top with remaining bagel half. Repeat with remaining egg mixture, bagels, cheese, tomato slices and lettuce. Serve immediately.

TIP: *If desired, omit tomato slices. Serve sandwich with prepared salsa.*

4 servings

TURKEY DINNER

For a large gathering, roast a whole bone-in turkey conventionally and microwave the side dishes. Much of the preparation can be done ahead to reduce last-minute fuss.

To serve a smaller group, microwave a boneless turkey. Although it is possible to microwave a bone-in turkey weighing under 11 pounds (5 kg), the boneless turkey requires less attention, is easier to carve and has no waste.

Turkey
page 180

Lemon Sage Dressing
page 181

Cranberry Waldorf Salad
page 181

Mashed Potatoes
with Turkey Gravy
page 181

Creamy Tarragon Peas &
Onions in Crispy Toast Cups
page 182

Rolls, Butter, Relishes

Orange Pumpkin Pie
page 183

179

TURKEY

- 16 to 20-lb. (7 to 9 kg) whole turkey, defrosted
- Salt and pepper
- 2 tablespoons to ¼ cup (25 to 50 mL) butter or margarine

16 to 20 servings

1 Heat conventional oven to 325°F/160°C. Rinse turkey and pat dry with paper towel. Sprinkle cavity lightly with salt and pepper. Secure legs together with string. Tuck wing tips under. Place turkey in large roasting pan.

2 Place butter in 1-cup (250 mL) measure. Microwave at High for 45 seconds to 1½ minutes, or until melted. Brush turkey with butter. Sprinkle outside of turkey with salt and pepper. Insert meat thermometer in thigh; cover with foil.

3 Estimate total cooking time at 20 to 30 minutes per pound (45 to 65 minutes per kilogram). Bake until internal temperature in inner thigh registers 185°F/85°C. During last 30 minutes, remove foil. Let stand, tented with foil, for 15 to 20 minutes before carving. Reserve drippings for gravy (opposite).

TURKEY GRAVY

- 2 cups (500 mL) reserved drippings
- ¼ cup (50 mL) all-purpose flour
- ¼ teaspoon (1 mL) salt
- Pinch pepper

2 cups (500 mL)

1 Strain drippings into 4-cup (1 L) measure. Add water or chicken broth, if necessary, to equal 2 cups (500 mL).

2 Place remaining ingredients in small mixing bowl. Add small amount of drippings to flour mixture. Stir until mixture is smooth. Add back to remaining drippings, stirring with whisk until smooth.

3 Microwave at High for 6 to 8 minutes, or until mixture thickens and bubbles, stirring 2 or 3 times.

LEMON SAGE DRESSING

- ½ cup (125 mL) butter or margarine
- 1 cup (250 mL) sliced celery
- ½ cup (125 mL) sliced green onions
- ½ cup (125 mL) shredded carrot
- 8 cups (2 L) unseasoned stuffing cubes
- 1½ cups (375 mL) ready-to-serve chicken broth
- ½ teaspoon (2 mL) grated lemon peel
- ½ teaspoon (2 mL) dried sage leaves
- ½ teaspoon (2 mL) salt
- ½ teaspoon (2 mL) pepper

8 servings

1 In large mixing bowl, microwave butter at High for 1½ to 1¾ minutes, or until melted. Add celery, onions and carrot. Cover with microwave-safe plastic wrap. Microwave at High for 3 to 4 minutes, or until vegetables are tender, stirring once.

2 Stir in remaining ingredients. Re-cover. * Microwave at High for 5 to 8 minutes, or until hot, stirring once or twice.

Advance preparation: *Up to 2 days in advance, prepare as directed to * above. Refrigerate. To serve, microwave at High, covered, for 9 to 12 minutes, or until hot, stirring once.*

CRANBERRY WALDORF SALAD

Dressing:
- 2 eggs
- ⅓ cup (75 mL) sugar
- ¼ cup (50 mL) orange juice
- 2 tablespoons (25 mL) water
- 2 tablespoons (25 mL) grated orange peel

Salad:
- 2 cups (500 mL) fresh or frozen cranberries, chopped
- 2 medium oranges, peeled and chopped (about 1 cup/250 mL)
- 1 large apple, chopped (about 1 cup/250 mL)
- 1 cup (250 mL) chopped dates
- ½ cup (125 mL) chopped walnuts
- 2 cups (500 mL) miniature marshmallows

8 servings

1 In 4-cup (1 L) measure, beat eggs well with whisk. Add remaining dressing ingredients. Beat with whisk until mixture is smooth. Microwave at 50% (Medium) for 4 to 6 minutes, or until mixture thickens, beating with whisk every 2 minutes. Chill about 2 hours, or until cold.

2 In large mixing bowl, combine salad ingredients. * Spoon dressing over salad. Toss gently to coat.

Advance preparation: *Up to 1 day in advance, prepare as directed to * above, except omit marshmallows. Cover and refrigerate dressing and salad in separate containers. To serve, add marshmallows to salad. Spoon dressing over salad. Toss gently to coat.*

CREAMY TARRAGON PEAS & ONIONS

- 1 tablespoon (15 mL) butter or margarine
- 1½ cups (375 mL) pearl onions, peeled
- 1½ cups (375 mL) frozen peas

Sauce:

- 2 tablespoons (25 mL) butter or margarine
- 1 tablespoon plus 1 teaspoon all-purpose flour (20 mL)
- ¼ teaspoon (1 mL) salt
- ¼ teaspoon (1 mL) grated lemon peel
- ⅛ teaspoon (0.5 mL) dried tarragon leaves
- Pinch white pepper
- 1 cup (250 mL) half-and-half

8 servings

Advance preparation: *Up to 2 days in advance, prepare onions and peas to * below. Cover and refrigerate. To serve, continue as directed.*

1 Place 1 tablespoon (15 mL) butter in 1½-quart (1.5 L) casserole. Microwave at High for 45 seconds to 1 minute, or until melted. Add onions. Cover. Microwave at High for 3 to 5 minutes, or until tender, stirring once. Stir in peas. * Set aside.

2 Place 2 tablespoons (25 mL) butter in 4-cup (1 L) measure. Microwave at High for 45 seconds to 1 minute, or until melted. Stir in remaining sauce ingredients, except half-and-half. Blend in half-and-half. Microwave at High for 3 to 4 minutes, or until mixture thickens and bubbles, stirring twice.

3 Pour sauce over peas and onions. Stir to blend. Microwave at High for 1 to 2 minutes, or until hot. Spoon evenly into Crispy Toast Cups (right), if desired.

CRISPY TOAST CUPS

- 8 slices soft white bread, crusts trimmed
- 2 tablespoons (25 mL) butter or margarine

8 servings

1 Heat oven to 350°F/180°C. Press each bread slice into ungreased muffin cup. In 1-cup (250 mL) measure, microwave butter at High for 45 seconds to 1 minute, or until melted. Brush bread with butter.

2 Bake for 20 to 25 minutes, or until light golden brown. Fill with creamed vegetables.

Advance preparation: *Up to 2 days in advance, prepare as directed above. Store in airtight container.*

ORANGE PUMPKIN PIE

- 1 pkg. (15 oz./425 g) refrigerated prepared pie crusts
- 2 teaspoons (10 mL) sugar
- 1¼ teaspoons (6 mL) ground cinnamon, divided
- 1 tablespoon (15 mL) milk
- Red and green candied cherries
- 1 can (16 oz./454 mL) pumpkin
- 1 can (14 oz./398 mL) sweetened condensed milk
- 2 eggs
- 1 teaspoon (5 mL) grated orange peel
- ¼ teaspoon (1 mL) ground nutmeg

8 servings

Advance preparation: *Up to 1 day in advance, prepare pie to * right and refrigerate. To serve, decorate with pastry bow.*

1 Heat oven to 425°F/220°C. Let pie crusts stand at room temperature for 15 to 20 minutes. Unfold 1 crust, ease into 9" (23 cm) pie plate and flute edges.

2 Combine sugar and ¼ teaspoon (1 mL) cinnamon in small bowl. Brush edges of crust lightly with milk. Sprinkle with about ½ teaspoon (2 mL) sugar mixture. Bake for 8 to 10 minutes, or until lightly browned. Cool.

3 Use remaining crust to form pastry bow and ribbon. Cut 4 strips, each 8" by ¾" (20 × 2 cm). Place 1 strip on baking sheet. Cross at center with another strip. Secure strips together, using a small amount of cold water.

4 Form bow over center of crossed strips, squeezing gently in center. Brush bow and ribbon lightly with milk. Sprinkle with remaining sugar mixture. Decorate center with red and green cherries. Bake at 425°F/220°C for 6 to 8 minutes, or until lightly browned. Cool.

5 Combine remaining 1 teaspoon (5 mL) cinnamon and the remaining ingredients in medium mixing bowl. Beat at low speed of electric mixer until mixture is smooth. Microwave at High for 4 to 5 minutes, or until mixture is very hot and starts to set, stirring once or twice.

6 Pour into prepared pie crust. Place pie plate on saucer in microwave oven. Microwave at 50% (Medium) for 15 to 21 minutes, or until center is set, rotating 3 or 4 times. * Using spatula, carefully loosen bow and ribbon from baking sheet. Place on top of filling. Cool.

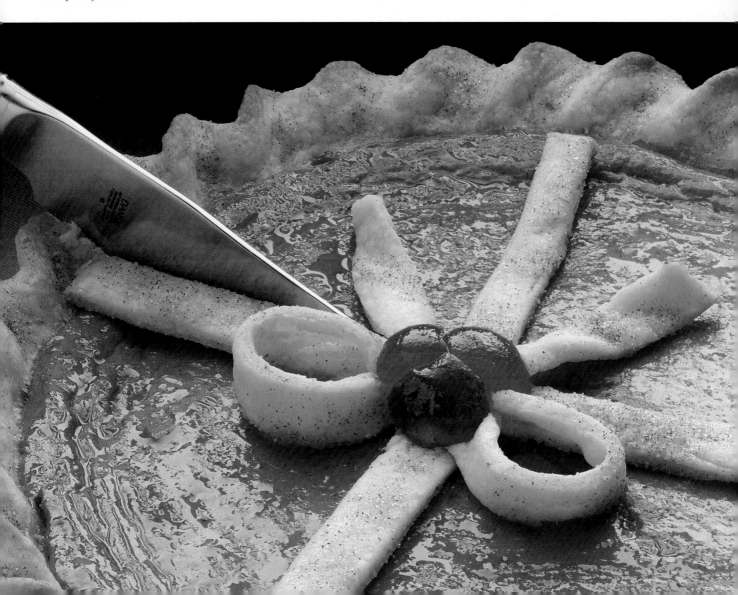

GLAZED HAM DINNER

Use the microwave oven to prepare ham for eight to ten people. When microwaved, a small boneless ham will be juicy. It is easier to roast a large ham conventionally when serving more than ten people.

Tangy Mustard-glazed Ham
opposite

Festive Melon Ball Mold
opposite

Candied Sweet Potatoes
opposite

Holiday Potato Scallop
opposite

Rolls, Butter, Relishes

Mincemeat Parfaits

TANGY MUSTARD-GLAZED HAM

- 1 cup (250 mL) packed brown sugar
- ¼ cup (50 mL) dry mustard
- ¼ cup (50 mL) apple or orange juice
- 8 to 10-lb. (4 to 5 kg) fully cooked boneless whole ham
- Whole cloves

16 to 20 servings

In small mixing bowl, combine all ingredients, except ham and cloves. Mix well. Set aside. Score and spice ham (below). Follow instructions for appropriate cooking method.

1 Prepare glaze (above). Set aside. Heat conventional oven to 325°F/160°C. Insert meat thermometer. Estimate total cooking time at 10 to 15 minutes per pound (25 to 35 minutes per kilogram). Place ham scored-side-up on rack in large roasting pan.

2 Brush with glaze during last 30 minutes of roasting time. Roast for remaining time, or until internal temperature registers 140°F/60°C, basting with drippings once.

3 Decorate ham with quartered orange slices during last 10 minutes, if desired. Secure orange pieces with cloves in diagonal lines. Baste ham with drippings and return to oven. Let stand for 10 minutes.

Scoring & Spicing Ham. Score top of ham in 1" (2.5 cm) diamond pattern, cutting ¼" (5 mm) deep. Insert 1 clove in center of each diamond.

HOLIDAY POTATO SCALLOP

- 6 cups (1.5 L) peeled, sliced potatoes (⅛"/3 mm slices)
- ¼ cup (50 mL) sliced green onions
- 3 tablespoons (50 mL) all-purpose flour
- ½ teaspoon (2 mL) salt
- ¼ teaspoon (1 mL) dried thyme leaves
- Pinch white pepper
- 2 cups (500 mL) half-and-half
- ⅓ cup (75 mL) snipped fresh parsley
- Sliced pimiento

6 to 8 servings

1 In 3-quart (3 L) casserole, combine all ingredients, except half-and-half, parsley and pimiento. Pour half-and-half over potato mixture. Toss gently to coat. Cover. Microwave at High for 6 minutes. Microwave at 50% (Medium) for 25 to 40 minutes longer, or until potatoes are tender and sauce is thickened, stirring twice.

2 Spoon potatoes into serving dish. Sprinkle parsley in wreath shape over potatoes. Arrange pimiento to form bow on wreath.

Holiday Au Gratin Potatoes: *Follow recipe above, except stir in 1 cup (250 mL) shredded Swiss cheese at end of cooking time. Cover. Let stand for 1 to 2 minutes, or until cheese melts.*

FESTIVE MELON BALL MOLD

- 1 cup (250 mL) hot water
- 1 pkg. (3 oz./85 g) lime gelatin
- ¾ cup (175 mL) cold water
- 2 cups (500 mL) cantaloupe balls
- 1 can (8 oz./227 mL) pineapple tidbits, drained
- 1 cup (250 mL) seedless red grapes
- ½ cup (125 mL) sliced celery
- Red-tipped leaf lettuce
- 1 pkg. (3 oz./85 g) cream cheese (optional)

8 servings

1 Brush the inside of 4 or 5-cup (1 L) mold lightly with vegetable oil. Set aside. Place hot water in 4-cup (1 L) measure. Cover with plastic wrap. Microwave at High for 2 to 3 minutes, or until boiling. Stir in gelatin until dissolved. Add cold water. Chill 1½ to 1¾ hours, or until gelatin is soft-set.

2 Add remaining ingredients, except lettuce and cream cheese. Pour into prepared mold. Chill 2 hours, or until set. * Arrange lettuce leaves on serving platter. Dip mold in hot water for 15 to 20 seconds. Loosen edges and unmold onto serving platter. Chill until serving time.

3 In small mixing bowl, microwave cream cheese at High for 15 to 30 seconds, or until softened. Stir until smooth. Spoon or pipe as desired onto salad.

Advance preparation: *Up to 1 day in advance, prepare mold to * above. Up to 4 hours in advance, unmold onto serving platter and decorate with cream cheese. Chill until serving time.*

CANDIED SWEET POTATOES

- 2 sweet potatoes (12 to 16 oz./375 to 500 g each), peeled and sliced
- 2 tablespoons (25 mL) butter or margarine
- ½ cup (125 mL) packed brown sugar
- 2 tablespoons (25 mL) light corn syrup
- 1 tablespoon (15 mL) unsweetened pineapple juice
- ⅛ teaspoon (0.5 mL) ground allspice
- 2 cups (500 mL) miniature marshmallows

6 to 8 servings

1 Arrange sweet potato slices, slightly overlapping, in 10" (25 cm) pie plate. Set aside. In 1-cup (250 mL) measure, microwave butter at High for 45 seconds to 1 minute, or until melted. Stir in remaining ingredients, except marshmallows. Pour evenly over potatoes. Cover with microwave-safe plastic wrap.

2 Microwave at High for 8 to 11 minutes, or until tender, rotating dish once. Remove plastic wrap. Sprinkle potatoes with marshmallows. Place under broiler, 8" (20 cm) from heat. Broil just until marshmallows are light golden brown, about 1 minute.

PORK CROWN ROAST DINNER

Because it requires a lot of attention, a pork crown roast is more suitable for conventional cooking. Roast it conventionally, then fill with a microwaved dressing. Serve with a broccoli & cauliflower ball decorated with lemon slices.

Pork Crown Roast with Fruit Glacé
below   *page 188*

Rice & Sausage Dressing
page 188

Sherried Sweet Potatoes
page 188

Broccoli & Cauliflower Ball

Strawberry-Avocado Salad
page 188

Rolls, Butter, Relishes

Pistachio-Cherry Cheesecake
page 189

PORK CROWN ROAST

- 1½ teaspoons (7 mL) fennel seed, crushed
- 1½ teaspoons (7 mL) onion powder
- 1 teaspoon (5 mL) salt
- 1 teaspoon (5 mL) pepper

- 8-lb. (4 kg) pork crown roast (about 16 ribs)
- Vegetable oil

8 to 10 servings

1 Combine all ingredients, except roast and oil, in small bowl. Rub mixture on all sides of roast. Cover and refrigerate overnight. Heat conventional oven to 325°F/160°C. Place roast on rack in roasting pan. Cover exposed bone ends with foil.

2 Brush roast lightly with oil. Insert meat thermometer. Estimate total cooking time at 20 minutes per pound (45 minutes per kilogram). Roast until internal temperature registers 165°F/72°C. Let stand for 10 minutes before carving.

FRUIT GLACÉ

- ½ cup (125 mL) dried apricot halves
- ½ cup (125 mL) dried calimyrna figs
- ½ cup (125 mL) dried peach halves
- ¾ cup (175 mL) apple juice, divided
- ¼ teaspoon (1 mL) ground cardamom
- 2 teaspoons (10 mL) cornstarch
- 1 cup (250 mL) seedless green grapes
- 1 cup (250 mL) seedless red grapes

6 to 8 servings

1 In 1½-quart (1.5 L) casserole, combine apricots, figs and peaches. Add ½ cup (125 mL) apple juice and the cardamom. Cover. Microwave at High for 5 to 8 minutes, or until fruits are plumped, stirring once.

2 In small bowl, combine cornstarch and remaining ¼ cup (50 mL) apple juice. Stir until smooth. Add to fruit mixture. Mix well. Microwave at High, uncovered, for 1½ to 2½ minutes, or until mixture is thickened and translucent, stirring once. Add grapes. Stir gently to coat. Spoon as garnish around Pork Crown Roast (page 187) or Tangy Mustard-Glazed Ham (page 185), if desired.

Advance preparation: Up to 2 days in advance, prepare as directed above and serve cold, if desired. To reheat, microwave at High, covered, for 1½ to 2½ minutes, or until hot, stirring once.

RICE & SAUSAGE DRESSING

- ½ cup (125 mL) butter or margarine
- ½ cup (125 mL) chopped onion
- ½ cup (125 mL) chopped green pepper
- ½ cup (125 mL) chopped carrot
- 4 cups (1 L) cooked long-grain white or brown rice
- 1 pkg. (8 oz./250 g) frozen, fully cooked pork sausage links, cut into ½" (1 cm) pieces
- ½ teaspoon (2 mL) salt
- ½ teaspoon (2 mL) dried thyme leaves
- ¼ teaspoon (1 mL) garlic powder
- Pinch pepper

8 servings

1 In large mixing bowl, microwave butter at High for 1½ to 1¾ minutes, or until melted. Add onion, green pepper and carrot. Cover with microwave-safe plastic wrap. Microwave at High for 3 to 4 minutes, or until vegetables are tender, stirring once.

2 Stir in remaining ingredients. Spoon into 2-quart (2 L) casserole. Re-cover. * Microwave at High for 7 to 9 minutes, or until hot, stirring once.

*Advance preparation: Up to 2 days in advance, prepare as directed to * above. Refrigerate. To serve, microwave at High for 10 to 12 minutes, or until hot, stirring once.*

SHERRIED SWEET POTATOES

- 2 cans (18 oz./511 mL each) sweet potatoes, drained
- ½ cup (125 mL) apricot nectar
- 2 eggs
- 2 tablespoons (25 mL) honey
- 2 tablespoons (25 mL) dry sherry
- ½ teaspoon (2 mL) salt
- ¼ teaspoon (1 mL) ground nutmeg
- ¼ cup (50 mL) chopped pecans

6 to 8 servings

1 In large mixing bowl, combine all ingredients, except pecans. Beat at medium speed of electric mixer until light and fluffy. Spread mixture in 10" (25 cm) pie plate. * Sprinkle evenly with pecans.

2 Cover with wax paper. Microwave at High for 4 minutes. Microwave at 50% (Medium) for 9 to 15 minutes longer, or until center is set, rotating dish once or twice.

*Advance preparation: Up to 2 days in advance, prepare sweet potato mixture to * above. Cover with plastic wrap and refrigerate. To serve, continue as directed, except microwave at 50% (Medium) for 12 to 20 minutes, or until center is set, rotating dish once or twice.*

STRAWBERRY-AVOCADO SALAD

- 6 cups (1.5 L) trimmed and torn curly endive
- 2 cups (500 mL) fresh strawberries, hulled and sliced
- 1 avocado, sliced

Dressing:
- ⅓ cup (75 mL) honey
- ⅓ cup (75 mL) orange juice
- ⅓ cup (75 mL) vegetable oil
- 1 tablespoon (15 mL) poppy seed

6 to 8 servings

In large mixing bowl, toss endive, strawberries and avocado. Set aside. In 2-cup (500 mL) measure, combine dressing ingredients. Microwave at High for 45 seconds to 1 minute, or until hot. Pour over endive mixture and toss to coat. Serve immediately.

Advance preparation: Up to 1 day in advance, combine dressing ingredients and refrigerate. To serve, toss endive, strawberries and avocado in large mixing bowl. Microwave dressing for 1½ to 2 minutes, or until hot. Pour over endive mixture and toss to coat.

PISTACHIO-CHERRY CHEESECAKE

Crust:

- ¼ cup (50 mL) butter or margarine
- 1 cup (250 mL) finely crushed chocolate wafer crumbs (about 20 wafers)

Filling:

- 1 pkg. (6 oz./170 g) white baking bar
- 2 pkgs. (8 oz./250 g each) cream cheese
- ⅔ cup (150 mL) sugar
- 2 egg whites
- 1 tablespoon (15 mL) all-purpose flour
- 1 teaspoon (5 mL) vanilla
- ½ cup (125 mL) chopped pistachio nuts
- ½ cup (125 mL) chopped candied cherries

8 to 10 servings

1 In 9" (23 cm) round baking dish, microwave butter at High for 1¼ to 1½ minutes, or until melted. Stir in wafer crumbs. Mix well. Press mixture firmly against bottom of dish. Microwave at High for 1½ to 2 minutes, or until set, rotating dish once. Set aside.

2 In small mixing bowl, microwave baking bar at 50% (Medium) for 4 to 5 minutes, or until bar melts and can be stirred smooth, stirring after the first 2 minutes and then every minute. Set aside.

3 In 2-quart (2 L) measure, microwave cream cheese at 50% (Medium) for 2¼ to 4 minutes, or until softened. Blend in melted baking bar. Add remaining filling ingredients, except pistachios and cherries. Beat at medium speed of electric mixer until well blended. Microwave at High for 2 minutes, or until mixture starts to set, beating with whisk every minute. Stir in pistachios and cherries.

4 Pour filling over prepared crust. Place dish on saucer in microwave oven. Microwave at 50% (Medium) for 7 to 10 minutes, or until cheesecake is set in center, rotating dish twice. (Filling becomes firm as it cools.) Refrigerate at least 8 hours, or overnight. Garnish with whole candied cherries, if desired.

Advance preparation: *Up to 2 days in advance, prepare as directed above. Cover with plastic wrap and refrigerate.*

HOT & SPICY PORK SALAD

- 2 tablespoons (25 mL) reduced-sodium soy sauce
- 1 tablespoon (15 mL) Chinese hot chili sauce with garlic
- 1-lb. (500 g) well-trimmed pork tenderloin, cut into 2" × ¼" (5 cm × 6 mm) strips
- 3 cups (750 mL) shredded leaf and Bibb lettuce
- 1 cup (250 mL) shredded green cabbage
- ½ cup (125 mL) shredded carrot
- ½ cup (125 mL) thinly sliced red pepper
- Unsalted peanuts (optional)

4 servings

1 Combine soy sauce and chili sauce in 1-cup (250 mL) measure. In small mixing bowl, combine pork strips and 1 tablespoon (15 mL) soy sauce mixture. Cover with plastic wrap. Chill 30 minutes.

2 Combine lettuce, cabbage, carrot and pepper in large mixing bowl or salad bowl. Toss to combine. Set aside.

3 Spray 10" (25 cm) nonstick skillet with nonstick vegetable cooking spray. Add pork. Cook over medium heat for 5 to 7 minutes, or just until meat is no longer pink, stirring occasionally. Drain. Add meat and remaining reserved soy sauce mixture to lettuce mixture. Toss to coat. Sprinkle with peanuts.

BARBECUED CHICKEN SANDWICH

- 1 small onion, sliced (½ cup/ 125 mL)
- ¼ cup (50 mL) chopped green pepper
- 1 clove garlic, minced
- 1 teaspoon (5 mL) olive oil
- 1 can (8 oz./227 mL) no-salt-added tomato sauce
- 3 tablespoons (50 mL) tomato paste
- 2 tablespoons (25 mL) packed brown sugar
- 1 tablespoon (15 mL) red wine vinegar
- 1 tablespoon (15 mL) Worcestershire sauce
- ½ teaspoon (2 mL) dry mustard
- 4 drops red pepper sauce
- 2 cups (500 mL) shredded cooked chicken, turkey or pork
- 4 whole wheat hamburger buns

4 servings

1 Place onion, green pepper, garlic and oil in 10" (25 cm) nonstick skillet. Cook over medium heat for 3 to 5 minutes, or until vegetables are tender, stirring frequently. Add remaining ingredients, except chicken and buns. Cook over medium heat for 5 minutes, or until barbecue sauce is slightly thickened and flavors are blended, stirring frequently.

2 Add shredded chicken to barbecue sauce. Cover. Cook over medium heat for 4 to 5 minutes, or until hot, stirring occasionally. Spoon ½ cup (125 mL) mixture onto each bun.

HEARTY VEGETABLE-BARLEY SOUP

- 3 cups (750 mL) water, divided
- 2 medium carrots, sliced (1 cup/ 250 mL)
- 1 stalk celery, sliced (½ cup/ 125 mL)
- ½ cup (125 mL) coarsely chopped green pepper
- 1 small onion, chopped (½ cup/ 125 mL)
- ½ cup (125 mL) sliced fresh mushrooms
- 1 can (14½ oz./411 g) diced tomatoes, undrained
- ½ cup (125 mL) uncooked quick-cooking barley
- 1 small zucchini, cut into ¼" (6 mm) slices (½ cup/125 mL)
- 1½ teaspoons (7 mL) instant beef bouillon granules
- 1 teaspoon (5 mL) dried rosemary leaves, crushed
- ½ teaspoon (2 mL) dried oregano leaves
- ½ teaspoon (2 mL) pepper

6 servings

1 Combine 1 cup (250 mL) water, the carrots, celery, green pepper, onion and mushrooms in 3-qt. (3 L) saucepan. Cover. Cook over high heat for 8 to 10 minutes, or until vegetables are tender, stirring occasionally.

2 Stir in remaining 2 cups (500 mL) water and remaining ingredients. Bring to a boil. Reduce heat to low. Simmer, uncovered, for 20 to 25 minutes, or until barley is tender, stirring occasionally.

Microwave Tip: *In 3-qt. (3 L) casserole, combine ¼ cup (50 mL) water, the carrots, celery, green pepper, onion and mushrooms. Cover. Microwave at High for 5 to 8 minutes, or until vegetables are tender, stirring once. Stir in remaining 2¾ cups (675 mL) water and remaining ingredients. Re-cover. Microwave at High for 25 to 30 minutes, or until barley is tender, stirring 2 or 3 times.*

192

CHICKEN DINNER SOUP

- 8 cups (2 L) water
- 3-lb. (1.5 kg) whole broiler-fryer chicken, quartered, skin removed
- 3 stalks celery, cut into 2" × ¼" (5 cm × 6 mm) strips (1½ cups/375 mL)
- 3 medium carrots, cut into 2" × ¼" (5 cm × 6 mm) strips (1½ cups/375 mL)
- 6 new potatoes, cut into ½" (1 cm) chunks (1½ cups/375 mL)
- 1 small leek, cut into 2" × ¼" (5 cm × 6 mm) strips (1 cup/250 mL)
- 1½ teaspoons (7 mL) dried tarragon leaves
- 1 to 1½ teaspoons (5 to 7 mL) freshly ground black pepper
- 1 teaspoon (5 mL) salt

10 servings

1 Combine water and chicken pieces in 6-qt. (6 L) Dutch oven or stockpot. Bring to a boil over high heat. Reduce heat to low. Cover. Simmer for 1 hour 15 minutes, skimming occasionally.

2 Remove chicken from broth. Chill broth, covered, at least 4 hours. Cut meat from bones. Discard bones. Coarsely shred chicken. Wrap in plastic wrap. Chill.

3 Skim and discard solidified fat from top of broth. Strain broth. In 6-qt. (6 L) Dutch oven or stockpot, combine broth, chicken and remaining ingredients. Bring to a boil over high heat. Reduce heat to medium-low. Simmer for 20 to 30 minutes, or until potatoes are tender.

HEARTY BEEF SKILLET MEAL →

- 1 pkg. (6¾ oz./190 g) quick-cooking long-grain white and wild rice mix
- 1 can (14½ oz./429 mL) ready-to-serve beef broth
- ¼ cup (50 mL) all-purpose flour
- ½ teaspoon (2 mL) salt
- ¼ teaspoon (1 mL) pepper
- 1 lb. (500 g) lean ground beef, crumbled
- 2 medium carrots, chopped (1 cup/250 mL)
- 1 medium onion, chopped (1 cup/250 mL)
- 1 cup (3 oz./85 g) sliced fresh mushrooms
- 1 stalk celery, sliced (½ cup/ 125 mL)
- 1 teaspoon (5 mL) dried thyme leaves
- 1 teaspoon (5 mL) dried basil leaves
- 1 teaspoon (5 mL) dried oregano leaves
- ½ teaspoon (2 mL) dried marjoram leaves
- 2 tablespoons (25 mL) snipped fresh parsley

6 servings

1 Prepare rice as directed on package, except discard seasoning packet and omit margarine and salt. Remove from heat. Cover to keep warm. Set aside.

2 Meanwhile, combine broth, flour, salt and pepper in 2-cup (500 mL) measure. Set aside. In 12" (30 cm) nonstick skillet, combine beef, carrots, onion, mushrooms, celery, thyme, basil, oregano, and marjoram. Cook over medium heat for 13 to 15 minutes, or until meat is no longer pink and vegetables are tender-crisp, stirring occasionally. Drain.

3 Add broth mixture to skillet. Cook over medium heat for 2 to 3 minutes, or until mixture thickens and bubbles, stirring constantly. Stir in rice. Cook for 1 to 2 minutes, or until heated through, stirring frequently. Remove from heat. Stir in parsley.

TURKEY TETRAZZINI ↑

- 8 oz. (227 g) uncooked spaghetti, broken into 2" (5 cm) lengths
- ¼ cup (50 mL) margarine, divided
- 1 cup (3 oz./85 g) sliced fresh mushrooms
- 1 stalk celery, sliced (½ cup/ 125 mL)
- 1 clove garlic, minced
- 3 tablespoons (50 mL) all-purpose flour
- 2½ cups (625 mL) skim milk
- ¼ teaspoon (1 mL) salt
- ¼ to ½ (1 to 2 mL) teaspoon pepper
- 1½ cups (375 mL) cubed fully cooked turkey breast or lean ham (¾"/2 cm cubes)
- ⅓ cup (75 mL) shredded low-fat Swiss cheese
- 1 jar (2 oz./50 g) sliced pimiento, drained

8 servings

1 Prepare spaghetti as directed on package. Rinse and drain. Set aside.

2 Heat oven to 350°F/180°C. In 2-qt. (2 L) saucepan, combine 1 tablespoon (15 mL) margarine, the mushrooms, celery and garlic. Cook over medium heat for 5 to 7 minutes, or until celery is tender-crisp, stirring occasionally. Stir in remaining 3 tablespoons (50 mL) margarine until melted. Stir in flour. Cook for 30 seconds to 1 minute, or until mixture bubbles.

3 Blend in milk, salt and pepper. Cook over medium heat for 10 minutes, stirring frequently. Reduce heat to low and cook for 2 to 5 minutes longer, or until sauce thickens and bubbles, stirring occasionally. In 2-qt. (2 L) casserole, combine sauce, spaghetti and remaining ingredients. Bake for 30 to 35 minutes, or until hot.

TANDOORI TURKEY & RICE

- 1 can (14½ oz./429 mL) ready-to-serve chicken broth
- 1 teaspoon (5 mL) chili powder
- ½ to 1 teaspoon (2 to 5 mL) ground cumin
- ¼ teaspoon (1 mL) ground turmeric
- ¼ teaspoon (1 mL) garlic powder
- Pinch white pepper
- 1½ cups (375 mL) uncooked instant brown rice

- 1 lb. (500 g) cooked turkey breast, cut into ½" (1 cm) cubes
- ½ cup (125 mL) red pepper strips (2" × ¼"/5 cm × 6 mm strips)
- 1 medium carrot, thinly sliced (½ cup/125 mL)
- 2 tablespoons (25 mL) snipped fresh cilantro or Italian parsley

6 servings

1 Combine broth, chili powder, cumin, turmeric, garlic powder and pepper in 12" (30 cm) nonstick skillet. Bring to a boil over high heat. Stir in rice. Cover. Reduce heat to low. Simmer for 5 minutes.

2 Stir in turkey, red pepper and carrot. Re-cover. Simmer for additional 5 to 6 minutes, or until turkey is hot and liquid is absorbed. Remove from heat. Stir in cilantro.

COUNTRY FRENCH SKILLET DINNER

- 1 teaspoon (5 mL) olive oil
- 2 boneless whole chicken breasts (8 to 10 oz./250 to 284 g each), split in half, skin removed, cut into 1½" × 1" (3.8 × 2.5 cm) pieces
- 8 oz. (250 g) fresh mushrooms, quartered (3 cups/750 mL)
- 2 cloves garlic, minced
- 1 cup (250 mL) ready-to-serve chicken broth
- 1 teaspoon (5 mL) Worcestershire sauce
- ½ teaspoon (2 mL) dried basil leaves
- ¼ teaspoon (1 mL) dried marjoram leaves
- ¼ teaspoon (1 mL) freshly ground pepper
- 1 lb. (500 g) small new potatoes, thinly sliced (3 cups/750 mL)
- 3 medium carrots, cut into 2" × ¼" (5 cm × 6 mm) strips (1½ cups/375 mL)
- ½ cup (125 mL) thinly sliced green onions

4 servings

1 Heat oil in 12" (30 cm) nonstick skillet over medium-high heat. Add chicken. Cook for 4 to 5 minutes, or just until lightly browned on all sides, stirring frequently.

2 Reduce heat to medium-low. Add mushrooms and garlic. Cook for 4 to 5 minutes, or until mushrooms are lightly browned, stirring frequently.

3 Stir in broth, Worcestershire sauce, basil, marjoram and pepper. Bring mixture to a boil over medium-high heat. Add potatoes and carrots. Reduce heat to medium-low. Cover. Simmer for 12 to 15 minutes, or until potatoes are tender. Stir in green onions.

CHICKEN & POTATO CASSEROLE

- 1 lb. (500 g) red or white potatoes, cut into ¼" (6 mm) slices (about 3 cups/750 mL)
- 1 cup (250 mL) water
- 3 whole boneless chicken breasts (8 to 10 oz./227 to 284 g each), skin removed, cut into 2" × ¼" (5 cm × 6 mm) strips
- 2 tablespoons (25 mL) margarine
- 3 tablespoons (50 mL) all-purpose flour
- 2 cups (500 mL) 1% low-fat milk
- 1 tablespoon (15 mL) snipped fresh parsley
- 1 teaspoon (5 mL) dried rubbed sage leaves
- 1 teaspoon (5 mL) dried thyme leaves
- ¾ teaspoon (4 mL) salt
- ¼ teaspoon (1 mL) white pepper
- 1 large red pepper, roasted*, peeled, seeded and cut into 1" (2.5 cm) chunks
- 1 tablespoon (15 mL) shredded fresh Parmesan cheese (optional)

6 servings

1 Spray 12" × 8" (30 × 46 cm) baking dish with non-stick vegetable cooking spray. Set aside. In 3-qt. (3 L) saucepan, combine potatoes and water. Cover. Cook over medium-high heat for 13 to 15 minutes, or just until potatoes are tender. Drain. Set aside.

2 Cook chicken over medium heat in 10" (25 cm) nonstick skillet for 6 to 8 minutes, or until meat is no longer pink, stirring frequently. Drain. Set aside.

3 Heat oven to 350°F/180°C. Melt margarine over medium heat in 1-qt. (1 L) saucepan. Stir in flour. Cook for 2 minutes, stirring constantly. Gradually blend in milk. Stir in parsley, sage, thyme, salt and white pepper. Cook for 5 to 10 minutes, or until sauce thickens and bubbles, stirring constantly. Remove from heat. Set aside.

4 Layer half of potatoes, half of chicken and half of pepper chunks in prepared dish. Repeat layers. Pour sauce evenly over top. Sprinkle evenly with Parmesan cheese. Bake for 20 to 25 minutes, or until casserole is hot and edges are bubbly.

*To roast pepper, place it under broiler with surface 1" to 2" (2.5 to 5 cm) from heat. Broil for 11 to 15 minutes, or until pepper blisters and blackens, turning pepper frequently. Place pepper in paper or plastic bag. Seal bag. Let stand for 10 minutes. Proceed as directed. If desired, use drained, jarred roasted red peppers.

198

ORANGE-SAUCED ROUGHY

- ½ cup (125 mL) fresh orange juice
- ⅓ cup (75 mL) ready-to-serve chicken broth or dry white wine
- 2 teaspoons (10 mL) cornstarch
- 1 teaspoon (5 mL) sugar
- ¼ teaspoon (1 mL) dried thyme leaves
- 1 lb. (500 g) orange roughy fillets, about ½" (1 cm) thick, cut into serving-size pieces
- 1 teaspoon (5 mL) vegetable oil

4 servings

1 Combine juice, broth, cornstarch, sugar and thyme in 1-qt. (1 L) saucepan. Cook over medium heat for 3 to 5 minutes, or until sauce is thickened and translucent, stirring constantly. Remove from heat. Set aside.

2 Heat broiler. Spray large baking sheet with nonstick vegetable cooking spray. Arrange fillets on sheet. Brush fillets evenly with oil.

3 Place under broiler with surface of fillets 5" (12.5 cm) from heat. Broil for 9 to 13 minutes, or until fish is firm and opaque and just begins to flake. Arrange fish on serving platter. Top with sauce.

Microwave Tip: *In 2-cup (500 mL) measure, combine juice, broth, corn-starch, sugar and thyme. Microwave at High for 2½ to 4½ minutes, or until sauce is thickened and translu-cent, stirring once or twice. Continue as directed.*

SPICY MANHATTAN CLAM CHOWDER

- 1 cup (250 mL) cubed red potatoes (¼"/6 mm cubes)
- ⅓ cup (75 mL) chopped onion
- ¼ cup (50 mL) grated carrot
- ¼ cup (50 mL) water
- 1 tablespoon (15 mL) margarine
- 2 cans (14½ oz./411 g each) whole tomatoes, undrained, cut up
- 1 can (6½ oz./184 g) minced clams, undrained
- ¾ cup (175 mL) spicy vegetable juice
- 2 tablespoons (25 mL) catsup
- 2 tablespoons (25 mL) snipped fresh parsley
- 1 bay leaf
- ¼ to ½ teaspoon (1 to 2 mL) red pepper sauce
- ¼ teaspoon (1 mL) dried thyme leaves
- Pinch pepper

1 Combine potatoes, onion, carrot, water and margarine in 3-qt. (3 L) saucepan. Cook over medium heat for 8 to 10 minutes, or until vegetables are tender, stirring frequently. (If vegetables begin to stick, add additional ¼ cup/50 mL water and continue cooking.)

2 Stir in remaining ingredients. Bring mixture to a boil over high heat. Cover. Reduce heat to low. Simmer for 10 to 15 minutes, or until chowder is hot and flavors are blended, stirring occasionally. Remove and discard bay leaf before serving.

Microwave Tip: *Omit water. In 2-qt. (2 L) casserole, combine potatoes, onion, carrot and margarine. Cover. Microwave at High for 5 to 6 minutes, or until vegetables are tender, stirring once. Stir in remaining ingredients. Re-cover. Microwave at 70% (Medium High) for 10 to 14 minutes, or until chowder is hot and flavors are blended, stirring once. Remove and discard bay leaf before serving.*

6 servings

THREE-CHEESE STUFFED MANICOTTI

- 8 uncooked manicotti shells
- 1¾ cups (425 mL) low-fat pasta sauce, divided
- 1 pkg. (9 oz./275 g) frozen chopped spinach, defrosted and well drained
- 1 cup (250 mL) low-fat or nonfat ricotta cheese
- 2 egg whites, slightly beaten
- 1 tablespoon (15 mL) shredded fresh Parmesan cheese
- ¼ teaspoon (1 mL) garlic powder
- ½ cup (125 mL) shredded part-skim mozzarella cheese

4 servings

1 Heat oven to 400°F/200°C. Prepare manicotti shells as directed on package. Rinse. Let stand in warm water.

2 Spread ¾ cup (175 mL) sauce in 12" × 8" (3 L) baking dish. Set aside.

3 Combine spinach, ricotta, egg whites, Parmesan cheese and garlic powder in medium mixing bowl. Drain shells. Stuff each shell with heaping ¼ cup (50 mL) spinach mixture. Arrange stuffed shells over sauce in baking dish.

4 Spoon remaining 1 cup (250 mL) sauce over shells. Cover with foil. Bake for 15 to 20 minutes, or until sauce bubbles. Sprinkle with mozzarella. Bake, uncovered, for 5 to 7 minutes, or until cheese is melted.

ZESTY BEEF CHILI ↑

- 1 lb. (454 g) beef stew meat, cut into ½" (1 cm) cubes
- 1 lb. (454 g) hot Italian sausage links, cut into ½" (1 cm) slices
- 2 medium onions, coarsely chopped (2 cups/500 mL)
- 6 cloves garlic, minced
- 1 can (28 oz./794 g) whole tomatoes, undrained and cut up
- 1 can (15 oz./425 g) tomato sauce
- ½ cup (125 mL) dry red wine
- ½ cup (125 mL) snipped fresh cilantro
- ¼ cup (50 mL) ground ancho chilies* (optional)
- 2 tablespoons (25 mL) sugar
- 1 tablespoon (15 mL) ground cocoa
- 1 tablespoon (15 mL) Worcestershire sauce
- 2 teaspoons (10 mL) dried oregano leaves
- 1 teaspoon (5 mL) ground cumin
- Hot pepper sauce
- 3 cans (16 oz./453 g each) pinto beans, rinsed and drained
- 1 large green pepper, coarsely chopped (1½ cups/375 mL)

8 to 10 servings

1 Combine beef, sausage, onions and garlic in 6 to 8-qt. (6 to 8 L) Dutch oven or stockpot. Cook over medium heat until beef and sausage are browned and onions are tender-crisp, stirring frequently.

2 Stir in tomatoes, tomato sauce, wine, cilantro, ancho chilies, sugar, cocoa, Worcestershire sauce, oregano and cumin. Bring to a simmer. Reduce heat to low. Simmer for 1 hour, stirring occasionally. Taste chili. Add hot pepper sauce to taste. Stir in beans and green pepper. Simmer for additional 30 minutes.

*Ancho chilies are dried poblano chiles. They are about 4" (10 cm) long and are a deep reddish brown, with a mild, rich flavor. They are available in Mexican or specialty markets.

WHITE CHICKEN CHILI

- 1 to 2 tablespoons (15 to 30 mL) olive oil
- 2 medium onions, chopped (2 cups/500 mL)
- 6 cloves garlic, minced
- 1 tablespoon (15 mL) ground cumin
- 2 teaspoons (10 mL) dried oregano leaves
- ¼ teaspoon (1 mL) ground cloves
- ¼ teaspoon (1 mL) cayenne (or more to taste)
- 4 cans (15½ oz./439 g each) Great Northern beans, rinsed and drained
- 6 cups (1.5 L) cubed cooked chicken breast*, ½" (1 cm) cubes
- 6 cups (1.5 L) chicken broth
- 2 cans (4 oz./113 g each) chopped mild green chilies
- 1 cup (250 mL) shredded Monterey Jack cheese

Toppings:
- Shredded Monterey Jack cheese
- Sour cream
- Mild green salsa

8 to 10 servings

1 Heat oil in 6 to 8-qt. (6 to 8 L) Dutch oven or stockpot. Add onions and garlic. Cook for 5 to 6 minutes, or until onions are tender, stirring frequently. Stir in cumin, oregano, cloves and cayenne. Cook for 1 minute, stirring frequently.

2 Stir in beans, chicken, broth and green chilies. Bring to a boil over medium-high heat. Reduce heat to low. Simmer for 1 hour, stirring occasionally. Stir in 1 cup (250 mL) cheese until melted. Serve chili with desired toppings.

*2 lbs. (907 g) fresh chicken breast will yield 6 cups (1.5 L) cubed chicken breast.

HOPPIN' JOHN

- 3 cups (750 mL) water
- 4 oz. (125 g) cubed fully cooked ham (¼"/6 mm cubes)
- 1 pkg. (10 oz./284 g) frozen black-eyed peas
- 1 cup (250 mL) uncooked long-grain white rice
- 1 medium onion, chopped (1 cup/250 mL)
- 1 cup (250 mL) chopped green pepper

- 2 cloves garlic, minced
- 1 teaspoon (5 mL) dried marjoram leaves
- ½ teaspoon (2 mL) salt
- ½ teaspoon (2 mL) cayenne
- ¼ teaspoon (1 mL) pepper
- 1 medium tomato, seeded and chopped (1 cup/250 mL)

6 servings

1 Combine water and ham in 3-qt. (3 L) saucepan. Bring to a boil over high heat. Add peas. Return to a boil. Cover. Reduce heat to low. Simmer for 15 minutes.

2 Stir in remaining ingredients, except tomato. Bring to a boil over high heat. Re-cover. Reduce heat to low. Simmer for 25 to 30 minutes, or until peas and rice are tender, stirring once. Stir tomato in during last 5 minutes of cooking.

← SOUR CREAM CUTOUTS

- 2 cups (500 mL) sugar
- 1 cup (250 mL) sour cream
- 3 eggs
- ½ cup (125 mL) butter or margarine, softened
- ½ cup (125 mL) vegetable shortening
- 5½ cups (1.375 L) all-purpose flour
- 2 teaspoons (10 mL) baking powder
- 2 teaspoons (10 mL) baking soda
- 1 teaspoon (5 mL) vanilla
- 1 teaspoon (5 mL) almond extract
- ¼ teaspoon (1 mL) salt
- Decorator frosting

About 10 dozen cookies

1 In large mixing bowl, combine sugar, sour cream, eggs, butter and shortening. Beat at medium speed of electric mixer until light and fluffy. Add flour, baking powder, baking soda, vanilla, almond extract and salt. Beat at low speed until soft dough forms. Cover with plastic wrap. Chill 1 to 2 hours, or until firm.

2 Heat oven to 350°F/180°C. On well-floured surface, roll dough to ¼" (5 mm) thickness. Using 3" (8 cm) cookie cutters, cut desired shapes into dough. Place shapes 2" (5 cm) apart on ungreased cookie sheets. Bake for 6 to 8 minutes, or until edges are light golden brown. Prepare frosting. Decorate cookies as desired. Let dry completely before storing.

SPECIAL-OCCASION SUGAR COOKIES

- 1 cup (250 mL) sugar
- ¾ cup (175 mL) butter or margarine, softened
- 1 egg
- 3 tablespoons (50 mL) whipping cream
- 1 teaspoon (5 mL) vanilla
- 1 teaspoon (5 mL) almond extract
- 3 cups (750 mL) all-purpose flour
- 1½ teaspoons (7 mL) baking powder
- ½ teaspoon (2 mL) salt
- Granulated sugar
- Decorator frosting

5½ dozen cookies

1 In large mixing bowl, combine 1 cup (250 mL) sugar, the butter, egg, whipping cream, vanilla and almond extract. Beat at medium speed of electric mixer until light and fluffy. Add flour, baking powder and salt. Beat at low speed until soft dough forms. Cover with plastic wrap. Chill 1 to 2 hours, or until firm.

2 Heat oven to 400°F/200°C. On floured surface, roll dough to ¼" (5 mm) thickness. Using 3" (8 cm) cookie cutters, cut desired shapes into dough. Place shapes 2" (5 cm) apart on ungreased cookie sheets. Sprinkle shapes with sugar. Bake for 4 to 6 minutes, or until edges are light golden brown. Prepare frosting. Decorate cookies as desired. Let dry completely before storing.

← POPPY SEED PINWHEELS

- ½ cup (125 mL) butter or margarine, softened
- ¼ cup (50 mL) granulated sugar
- 1 egg
- 1 teaspoon (5 mL) grated orange peel
- 1 teaspoon (5 mL) vanilla
- 1½ cups (375 mL) all-purpose flour
- ½ teaspoon (2 mL) baking soda
- 1 cup (250 mL) poppy seed filling, divided
- Powdered sugar (optional)

4 dozen cookies

1 In large mixing bowl, combine butter, granulated sugar, egg, peel and vanilla. Beat at medium speed of electric mixer until light and fluffy. Add flour and bak-ing soda. Beat at low speed until soft dough forms. Divide dough in half. Cover with plastic wrap. Chill 30 minutes to 1 hour, or until firm.

2 Roll half of dough between 2 sheets of wax paper into 12" x 10" (30 x 25 cm) rectangle. Repeat with remaining dough. Chill 30 minutes.

3 Heat oven to 350°F/180°C. Lightly grease cookie sheets. Set aside. Discard top sheet of wax paper from first half dough. Spread ½ cup (125 mL) fill-ing to within ¼" (5 mm) of edges. Roll dough jelly roll style, starting with long side. (Peel off wax paper when rolling.) Pinch edge to seal. Repeat with remaining dough and ½ cup (125 mL) filling.

4 Cut rolls into ½" (1 cm) slices. Place slices 2" (5 cm) apart on prepared cookie sheets. Bake for 10 to 12 minutes, or until edges are light golden brown. Cool completely. Sprinkle pinwheels with powdered sugar.

Optional Glaze:

- 1 cup (250 mL) powdered sugar
- 1 to 2 tablespoons (15 to 25 mL) orange juice

In small mixing bowl, combine sugar and juice. Stir until smooth. Drizzle over cooled pinwheels.

← HOLIDAY THUMBPRINT COOKIES

- 1 cup (250 mL) butter or margarine, softened
- ½ cup (125 mL) packed brown sugar
- 2 eggs, separated
- 2 cups (500 mL) all-purpose flour
- 1 teaspoon (5 mL) water
- 1½ cups (375 mL) finely chopped pecans
- 3 tablespoons (50 mL) currant jelly or other tart jelly

3 dozen cookies

1 Heat oven to 300°F/150°C. In large mixing bowl, combine butter, sugar and egg yolks. Beat at medium speed of electric mixer until light and fluffy. Add flour. Beat at low speed until soft dough forms. Set aside.

2 In small mixing bowl, beat egg whites and water at high speed until foamy. Set aside.

3 Shape dough into 1" (2.5 cm) balls. Dip balls into egg white mixture. Roll balls in pecans. Place balls 2" (5 cm) apart on ungreased cookie sheets. Indent top of each cookie with thumb. Bake for 18 to 20 minutes, or until set.

4 Immediately indent cookies again. Spoon ¼ teaspoon (1 mL) jelly into each thumbprint. Cool completely before storing. (Do not stack cookies.)

TIP: *Use end of spoon to make indentation in hot cookies.*

BRANDIED GINGER SNAPS

- ½ cup (125 mL) granulated sugar
- ½ cup (125 mL) butter or margarine
- ⅓ cup (75 mL) dark molasses
- 1 tablespoon (15 mL) apricot-flavored brandy
- 1¾ to 2 cups (425 to 500 mL) all-purpose flour, divided
- 1 teaspoon (5 mL) pumpkin pie spice
- Pinch salt

Frosting:

- 2 cups (500 mL) powdered sugar
- ¼ cup (50 mL) caramel ice cream topping
- 1 to 2 teaspoons (5 to 10 mL) milk
- ½ teaspoon (2 mL) vanilla

About 3½ dozen cookies

1 Heat oven to 350°F/ 180°C. Lightly grease cookie sheets. Set aside. In 1-quart (1 L) saucepan, combine gran-ulated sugar, butter and molasses. Bring to boil over medium heat, stirring constantly. Boil for 1 minute. Remove from heat. Stir in brandy. Set aside.

2 In large mixing bowl, combine 1¼ cups (300 mL) flour, the pumpkin pie spice and salt. Add butter mixture. Beat at medium speed of electric mixer until well blended. Stir or knead in enough of remaining ¾ cup (175 mL) flour to form stiff dough.

3 On prepared cookie sheet, roll out two-thirds dough to ⅛" to ¼" (3 to 5 mm) thickness. Using 3" (8 cm) star-shaped cookie cutter, cut shapes into dough at ½" (1 cm) intervals. Remove scraps and knead into remaining dough. Repeat with remain-ing dough on additional prepared cookie sheets. Bake for 7 to 8 minutes, or until set. Cool completely.

4 In small mixing bowl, combine frosting ingredients. Beat at high speed of electric mixer until smooth. Pipe star outline on cookies, or frost cookies with thin layer of frosting. Let dry completely before storing.

APPLIQUÉD ALMOND COOKIES

- ¾ cup (175 mL) butter or margarine, softened
- ⅓ cup (75 mL) almond paste
- 1 cup (250 mL) granulated sugar
- 1 egg
- 3 tablespoons (50 mL) milk
- 1 teaspoon (5 mL) almond extract

- 3 cups (750 mL) all-purpose flour
- 1½ teaspoons (7 mL) baking powder
- ½ teaspoon (2 mL) salt
- Food coloring
- Coarse sugar crystals

6 dozen cookies

1 In large mixing bowl, combine butter and almond paste. Beat at medium speed of electric mixer until smooth. Add granulated sugar, egg, milk and almond extract. Beat at medium speed until well blended. Add flour, baking powder and salt. Beat at low speed until soft dough forms. Divide dough into thirds. Cover ⅔ dough with plastic wrap. Add food coloring, one drop at a time, to remaining ⅓ dough, kneading dough until color is equally distributed and dough is desired shade. Cover with plastic wrap. Chill all dough 2 to 3 hours, or until firm.

2 Heat oven to 400°F/200°C. On floured surface, roll half of uncolored dough to ⅛" (3 mm) thickness. Using 2¼" (6 cm) round cookie cutter, cut circles into dough. Place circles 2" (5 cm) apart on ungreased cookie sheets. Set aside.

3 On floured surface, roll half of colored dough to ⅛" (3 mm) thickness. Using 2" (5 cm) cutter of desired shape (see Decorating Tip), cut shapes into dough. Place one colored shape on top of each uncolored circle. Repeat with remaining colored and uncolored dough. Sprinkle shapes with sugar crystals. Bake for 5 to 7 minutes, or until edges are golden brown. Cool completely before storing.

LEMON BLOSSOM SPRITZ ↑

- 1 cup (250 mL) butter or margarine, softened
- ½ cup (125 mL) granulated sugar
- ½ cup (125 mL) packed brown sugar
- 1 egg
- 1 teaspoon (5 mL) grated lemon peel
- 1 tablespoon (15 mL) fresh lemon juice
- 1 teaspoon (5 mL) vanilla
- 2½ cups (625 mL) all-purpose flour

- ¼ teaspoon (1 mL) baking soda
- ¼ teaspoon (1 mL) salt

Frosting:

- 1¼ cups (300 mL) powdered sugar
- ½ teaspoon (2 mL) grated lemon peel
- 2 to 4 teaspoons (10 to 20 mL) fresh lemon juice
- ½ teaspoon (2 mL) vanilla

About 5 dozen cookies

1 In large mixing bowl, combine butter, granulated sugar, brown sugar, egg, 1 teaspoon (5 mL) peel, 1 tablespoon (15 mL) juice and 1 teaspoon (5 mL) vanilla. Beat at medium speed of electric mixer until light and fluffy. Add flour, baking soda and salt. Beat at low speed until soft dough forms. Cover with plastic wrap. Chill 1 to 2 hours, or until firm.

2 Heat oven to 400°F/200°C. Place dough in cookie press. Using flower-patterned plate, press cookies 2" (5 cm) apart onto ungreased cookie sheets. Bake for 5 to 7 minutes, or until edges are light golden brown. Cool completely.

3 In small mixing bowl, combine frosting ingredients. Beat at low speed of electric mixer until smooth. Spread frosting evenly on cookies. Let dry completely before storing.

COCOA PEPPERMINT PRETZELS →

- 1 cup (250 mL) powdered sugar
- 1 cup (250 mL) butter or margarine, softened
- 1 egg
- 1½ teaspoons (7 mL) vanilla
- 2½ cups (625 mL) all-purpose flour

- ½ cup (125 mL) unsweetened cocoa
- ½ teaspoon (2 mL) salt
- ½ cup (125 mL) vanilla baking chips
- 1 teaspoon (5 mL) vegetable shortening
- 12 hard peppermint candies, crushed

4 dozen cookies

1 In large mixing bowl, combine sugar, butter, egg and vanilla. Beat at medium speed of electric mixer until light and fluffy. Add flour, cocoa and salt. Beat at low speed until soft dough forms. Cover with plastic wrap. Chill 2 to 3 hours, or until firm.

2 Heat oven to 375°F/190°C. Shape level measuring tablespoons (15 mL) dough into 9"-long (23 cm) ropes. Twist ropes into pretzel shapes. Place pretzels 2" (5 cm) apart on ungreased cookie sheets. Bake for 8 to 9 minutes, or until set. Cool completely.

3 Line cookie sheets with wax paper. Set aside. In 1-quart (1 L) saucepan, combine chips and shortening. Melt over low heat, stirring constantly. Dip one end of each pretzel into melted chips, then roll dipped ends into crushed candies. Place pretzels on prepared cookie sheets. Let dry completely before storing.

MICROWAVE TIP: *In small mixing bowl, melt chips and shortening at 50% (Medium) for 2 to 4 minutes, stirring after every minute. Continue as directed.*

← MINT TRUFFLE COOKIES

- 1¼ cups (300 mL) sugar
- 1 cup (250 mL) butter or margarine, softened
- 2 eggs
- 1 teaspoon (5 mL) vanilla
- 2½ cups (625 mL) all-purpose flour
- ¼ cup (50 mL) unsweetened cocoa
- 1 teaspoon (5 mL) baking powder
- ¼ teaspoon (1 mL) salt

- 1 pkg. (4.67 oz./132 g) chocolate sandwich mints, coarsely chopped

Glaze

- 8 oz. (250 g) white candy coating
- 1 teaspoon (5 mL) vegetable shortening
- 1 or 2 drops green food coloring

4 dozen cookies

1 In large mixing bowl, combine sugar, butter, eggs and vanilla. Beat at medium speed of electric mixer until light and fluffy. Add flour, cocoa, baking powder and salt. Beat at low speed until soft dough forms. Stir in mints. Cover with plastic wrap. Chill 2 to 3 hours, or until firm.

2 Heat oven to 375°F/190°C. Lightly grease cookie sheets. Shape dough into 1" (2.5 cm) balls. Place balls 2" (5 cm) apart on prepared cookie sheets. Bake for 8 to 10 minutes, or until set. Cool completely.

3 In 1-quart (1 L) saucepan, combine candy coating and shortening. Melt over low heat, stirring constantly. Stir in food coloring. Pipe or drizzle glaze over cookies to form stripes. Let dry completely before storing.

MICROWAVE TIP: *In small mixing bowl, melt candy coating and shortening at 50% (Medium) for 2 to 4 minutes, stirring after every minute. Continue as directed.*

← CHOCOLATE-DIPPED HAZELNUT BISCOTTI

- 1 cup (250 mL) slivered almonds
- 1½ cups (375 mL) sugar
- ½ cup (125 mL) unsalted butter, softened
- 2 tablespoons (25 mL) hazelnut liqueur
- 3 eggs
- 3¾ cups (925 mL) all-purpose flour
- 2 teaspoons (10 mL) baking powder
- Pinch salt
- 1 cup (250 mL) milk chocolate chips
- 2 teaspoons (10 mL) vegetable shortening
- 1½ cup (125 mL) finely chopped hazelnuts

3½ dozen cookies

1 Heat oven to 350°F/180°C. Lightly grease cookie sheets. Set aside. Place almonds in 8" (2 L) square baking pan. Bake for 10 to 12 minutes, or until light golden brown, stirring occasionally. Coarsely chop almonds. Set aside.

2 In large mixing bowl, combine sugar, butter and liqueur. Beat at medium speed of electric mixer until light and fluffy. Add eggs, one at a time, beating after each addition. Add flour, baking powder and salt. Beat at low speed until soft dough forms. Stir in almonds.

3 Divide dough into quarters. On lightly floured surface, shape each quarter into 2"-diameter (5 cm) log. Place logs 2" (5 cm) apart on prepared cookie sheet. Bake for 30 to 35 minutes, or until golden brown.

4 Immediately cut logs diagonally into ¾" (2 cm) slices. Place slices 1" (2.5 cm) apart on prepared cookie sheets. Bake for additional 10 to 15 minutes, or until dry and golden brown. Cool completely.

5 In 1-quart (1 L) saucepan, combine chips and shortening. Melt over low heat, stirring constantly. Remove from heat. Dip one end of each cookie diagonally into melted chocolate. Sprinkle hazelnuts evenly over dipped ends. Let dry completely before storing.

← STAINED GLASS COOKIES

- 1 cup (250 mL) sugar
- ½ cup (125 mL) butter or margarine, softened
- ⅓ cup (75 mL) vegetable shortening
- 2 eggs
- 1 teaspoon (5 mL) grated orange peel
- 1 teaspoon (5 mL) vanilla
- 2¾ cups (675 mL) all-purpose flour
- 1 teaspoon (5 mL) baking powder
- 1 teaspoon (5 mL) salt
- 5 rolls (.9 oz./22 g each) ring-shaped hard candies (assorted flavors)

4 dozen cookies

1 In large mixing bowl, combine sugar, butter and shortening. Beat at medium speed of electric mixer until light and fluffy. Add eggs, peel and vanilla. Beat at medium speed until well blended. Add flour, baking powder and salt. Beat at low speed until soft dough forms. Cover with plastic wrap. Chill 1 to 2 hours, or until firm.

2 Heat oven to 350°F/180°C. Line cookie sheets with foil. Set aside. Divide dough into thirds. On well-floured surface, roll one third dough to ¼" (5 mm) thickness. Using 3" (8 cm) cookie cutters, cut desired shapes into dough. Place shapes 2" (5 cm) apart on prepared cookie sheets.

3 Using smaller cookie cutters, straws or a sharp knife, cut desired shapes out of cookies on cookie sheets. (If cookies are to be hung as ornaments, make a small hole at the top of each cookie for string.) Repeat with remaining dough.

4 Place like-colored candies in small plastic bags. Coarsely crush candies by tapping each bag with back of large spoon. Fill cutout areas of cookies to the top with candies. Bake for 7 to 9 minutes, or until edges are light golden brown and candies are melted. Cool completely before removing from foil. Gently pull cookies off foil.

APRICOT-DATE BALLS (top)

- ¾ cup (175 mL) sugar
- ½ cup (125 mL) chopped dried apricots
- ½ cup (125 mL) chopped dates
- 2 eggs, beaten
- 1 cup (250 mL) finely chopped walnuts
- 1 teaspoon (5 mL) vanilla
- Granulated sugar

4 dozen cookies

1 Line airtight container with wax paper. Set aside. In 2-quart (2 L) saucepan, combine ¾ cup (175 mL) sugar, the apricots, dates and eggs. Cook over low heat for 6 to 8 minutes, or until mixture pulls away from side of pan, stirring constantly.

2 Remove from heat. Stir in walnuts and vanilla. Let stand for 45 to 50 minutes, or until mixture is cool enough to handle.

3 Shape mixture into 1" (2.5 cm) balls. Roll balls in sugar. Place balls in prepared container. Store in refrigerator.

SPICY GREEK JEWELS (bottom)

- 2 cups (500 mL) powdered sugar
- 1 cup (250 mL) butter or margarine, softened
- 1 egg
- 2½ cups (625 mL) all-purpose flour
- 1½ cups (375 mL) ground almonds
- 1½ teaspoons (7 mL) apple pie spice
- ¼ teaspoon (1 mL) salt
- Powdered sugar
- 24 red candied cherries, halved
- 12 green candied pineapple chunks, each cut into 8 pieces

4 dozen cookies

1 Heat oven to 350°F/180°C. In large mixing bowl, combine 2 cups (500 mL) powdered sugar, the butter and egg. Beat at medium speed of electric mixer until light and fluffy. Add flour, almonds, apple pie spice and salt. Beat at low speed until soft dough forms.

2 Shape dough into 1" (2.5 cm) balls. Place balls 2" (5 cm) apart on ungreased cookie sheets. Flatten to ¼" (5 mm) thickness with bottom of drinking glass, dipping glass in powdered sugar to prevent sticking.

3 Decorate each cookie with 1 cherry half and 2 pineapple pieces, pressing fruit lightly into dough. Bake for 12 to 14 minutes, or until edges are golden brown. Cool completely before storing.

CRUNCHY COFFEE FROZEN TORTE

- ¼ cup (50 mL) hot water
- 2 tablespoons (25 mL) instant coffee crystals
- 1 quart (0.9 L) vanilla nonfat frozen yogurt or low-fat ice cream
- 8 chocolate sandwich cookies, coarsely chopped

10 servings

1 Combine water and coffee crystals in 1-cup (250 mL) measure. Set aside. Place frozen yogurt in medium mixing bowl. Let soften until yogurt can be stirred smooth. Add coffee and chopped cookies. Mix well.

2 Spoon mixture evenly into 8" (20 cm) springform pan. Freeze 4 hours, or until firm. Cut torte into wedges. Garnish with nonfat whipped topping and maraschino cherries, if desired.

PEAR NAPOLEONS IN RASPBERRY SAUCE

- 1 pkg. (10 oz./284 g) frozen raspberries in light syrup, defrosted
- ¼ cup plus 3 tablespoons (100 mL) sugar, divided
- 1 teaspoon (5 mL) cornstarch
- ¼ cup (50 mL) sour cream
- 3 tablespoons (50 mL) honey
- ½ teaspoon (2 mL) almond extract
- 18 wonton skins
- 6 small d'Anjou pears (5 to 6 oz./150 to 175 g each)
- 1 cup (250 mL) water mixed with 1 tablespoon (15 mL) lemon juice
- 1 tablespoon (15 mL) sugar mixed with ½ teaspoon (2 mL) ground cinnamon
- 2 tablespoons (25 mL) finely chopped almonds (optional)

6 servings

1 Heat oven to 375°F/190°C. Line 2 baking sheets with parchment paper. Set aside. In food processor or blender, process raspberries until smooth. Strain through fine-mesh sieve. Discard seeds. In 1-qt. (1 L) saucepan, combine 2 tablespoons (25 mL) sugar and the cornstarch. Blend in raspberry juice. Bring to a boil over medium heat, stirring frequently. Remove from heat. Set sauce aside. In small bowl, combine sour cream, honey and almond extract. Cover filling with plastic wrap. Chill.

2 Place ¼ cup plus 1 tablespoon (65 mL) sugar in shallow dish. Spray both sides of each wonton skin with nonstick vegetable cooking spray. Press both sides into sugar. Place on prepared baking sheets. Bake for 7 to 10 minutes, or until edges are golden brown, turning wonton skins over after half the time. Transfer wonton skins to cooling racks. Set aside.

3 Reduce oven temperature to 350°F/180°C. Line 2 baking sheets with fresh parchment paper. Set aside. Peel, core and halve each pear. Immerse halves in water and lemon juice mixture. Cut halves lengthwise into ⅛" (3 mm) thick slices. Place halves on prepared baking sheets, fanning slices slightly. Sprinkle sugar and cinnamon mixture evenly over pears. Bake for 15 to 19 minutes, or until pears are tender.

4 Place 1 wonton skin on each serving plate. Arrange one-third of pear slices evenly on wonton skins. Top each with rounded teaspoon (5 mL) filling. Top each with second wonton skin. Arrange one-third of pear slices on second wonton skins, fanning slices into circles, with holes in centers. Fill each hole with rounded teaspoon (5 mL) filling. Top each with third wonton skin. Arrange remaining pear slices evenly on third wonton skins. Spoon about 2 tablespoons (25 mL) raspberry sauce over and around each napoleon. Sprinkle almonds evenly over napoleons. Garnish with fresh raspberries and fresh mint sprigs, if desired.

OATMEAL FRUIT CRISP ↑

Filling:

- 3 cups (750 mL) sliced peeled fresh peaches, pears or apples
- ¼ cup (50 mL) sugar
- 1 tablespoon (15 mL) all-purpose flour

Topping:

- ⅓ cup (75 mL) uncooked quick-cooking oats
- 3 tablespoons (50 mL) packed brown sugar
- 2 tablespoons (25 mL) all-purpose flour
- ½ teaspoon (2 mL) ground cinnamon
- ¼ teaspoon (1 mL) salt
- 2 tablespoons (25 mL) cold margarine or butter, cut into pieces

6 servings

1 Heat oven to 375°F/190°C. Spray 8" (2 L) square baking pan with nonstick vegetable cooking spray. Set aside.

2 Combine filling ingredients in medium mixing bowl. Spoon filling into prepared pan. In small mixing bowl, combine oats, brown sugar, flour, cinnamon and salt. Cut in margarine until mixture resembles coarse crumbs. Sprinkle topping evenly over filling. Bake for 30 to 35 minutes, or until hot and edges are bubbly. Serve warm with low-fat vanilla ice cream, if desired.

PHYLLO APPLE TURNOVER →

Filling:

- 2 medium Granny Smith apples, peeled, cored and thinly sliced (3 cups/750 mL)
- ¼ cup (50 mL) dried currants
- ¼ cup (50 mL) sugar
- 1 tablespoon (15 mL) all-purpose flour
- ½ teaspoon (2 mL) ground cinnamon

- 2 tablespoons (25 mL) sugar
- ¼ teaspoon (1 mL) ground cinnamon
- 12 sheets frozen phyllo dough, defrosted
- 1 teaspoon (5 mL) margarine, melted

6 servings

1 Heat oven to 375°F/190°C. In medium mixing bowl, combine filling ingredients. Set aside. In small mixing bowl, combine 2 tablespoons (25 mL) sugar and ¼ teaspoon (1 mL) cinnamon. Set aside.

2 Place 1 sheet of phyllo on flat work surface. (Keep remaining sheets covered with plastic wrap.) Spray sheet evenly with nonstick vegetable cooking spray. Lay second sheet of phyllo over first. Spray second sheet evenly with cooking spray. Cut layered sheets in half lengthwise. Lay one half of cut sheets on second half, forming 4 layers.

3 Place ½ cup (125 mL) filling at one end of layered sheets. Fold right bottom corner over filling, forming a triangle. Continue folding, keeping triangle shape. Place triangle seam-side-down on baking sheet. Repeat with remaining phyllo sheets and filling.

4 Brush tops of triangles with margarine. Sprinkle evenly with sugar mixture. Bake for 15 to 18 minutes, or until turnovers are golden brown. Serve with low-fat praline and caramel ice cream, if desired.

← FRUIT PIZZA

- ½ pkg. (20 oz./625 g) refrigerated sugar cookie dough
- ½ cup (125 mL) apricot jam
- 1 pkg. (8 oz./250 g) low-fat cream cheese, softened
- ¼ cup (50 mL) powdered sugar
- 5 cups (1.25 L) assorted chopped or sliced fruit (kiwifruit, pineapple, mandarin oranges, grapes, strawberries, bananas)

10 servings

1 Heat oven to 350°F/180°C. Shape dough into ball. With lightly floured hands, press dough evenly into 12" (30 cm) round pizza pan. Bake for 9 to 11 minutes, or until crust is lightly browned. Cool completely.

2 Melt jam in 1-qt. (1 L) saucepan over medium-low heat, stirring occasionally. Strain. Cool slightly. Set glaze aside.

3 Combine cheese and sugar in medium mixing bowl. Beat at low speed of electric mixer until smooth, scraping sides of bowl frequently. Spread cream cheese mixture evenly over crust to within ½" (1 cm) of edges.

4 Arrange fruit decoratively over cheese mixture. Spoon glaze evenly over fruit. Chill 30 to 40 minutes, or until set. Cut into 10 wedges to serve.

TIP: *Individual servings of pizza are easy to transfer to serving plate. However, the crust may break if pizza is transferred whole.*

FUDGE-MINT DESSERT ↑

Crust:
- ½ pkg. (1 lb. 4½ oz./635 g) low-fat fudge brownie mix (about 2 packed cups/500 mL)
- ⅓ cup (75 mL) hot water
- 2 egg whites, beaten
- 1 teaspoon (5 mL) vanilla

Filling:
- ¾ cup (175 mL) cold skim milk
- 1 pkg. (3.9 oz./120 g) instant chocolate pudding mix
- 2 tablespoons (25 mL) clear crème de menthe
- 1 teaspoon (5 mL) vanilla
- 1½ cups (375 mL) frozen reduced-calorie nondairy whipped topping, defrosted

Topping:
- 1½ cups (375 mL) frozen reduced-calorie nondairy whipped topping, defrosted
- 2 teaspoons (10 mL) clear crème de menthe
- 1 to 2 drops green food coloring (optional)
- 1 tablespoon (15 mL) miniature chocolate chips

9 servings

1 Heat oven to 325°F/160°C. Spray 9" (2.5 L) square baking pan with nonstick vegetable cooking spray. Set aside.

2 Combine crust ingredients in medium mixing bowl. Beat at low speed of electric mixer just until smooth, scraping sides of bowl frequently. Pour crust into prepared pan. Bake for 20 to 22 minutes, or until set. (Do not overbake.) Cool completely.

3 Combine milk, pudding mix, 2 tablespoons (25 mL) crème de menthe and the vanilla in second medium mixing bowl. Beat at low speed of electric mixer for 1 minute, scraping sides of bowl frequently. Fold in 1½ cups (375 mL) whipped topping. Spread filling evenly over crust.

4 Place 1½ cups (375 mL) whipped topping in small mixing bowl. Fold in 2 teaspoons (10 mL) crème de menthe and the food coloring. Spread topping evenly over filling. Sprinkle chips evenly over top. Cover with plastic wrap. Chill. Cut into 9 squares to serve.

INDEX

Creative Publishing international, Inc.
offers a variety of how-to books. For
information write:
    Creative Publishing international, Inc.
    Subscriber Books
    5900 Green Oak Drive
    Minnetonka, MN 55343